Betta
Handbook

Robert J. Goldstein, Ph.D.
Filled with Full-color Photographs

BARRON'S

About the Author

Dr. Robert J. Goldstein received his Ph.D. at the University of Texas Southwestern Medical School, his M.Sc. at Florida State, and his B.Sc. at Brooklyn College. He is currently president of an environmental consulting firm in Raleigh, N.C., where he resides with his wife Dr. Joyce Goldstein, a scientist at the National Institute of Environmental Health Sciences.

He has been writing books and magazine articles for over thirty years, with credits in *Sports Afield, Outside, Field & Stream, Fishing World, North Carolina Sportsman, Florida Sportsman, Pesces, Pet Age, Tropical Fish Hobbyist, Aquarist and Pondkeeper, DATZ,* and *Das Aquarium.* His books include *Cichlids, Introduction to the Cichlids, Cichlids of the World, Diseases of Aquarium Fishes, Anabantoids, Bettas, Angelfishes, Marine Aquarium Handbook, Coastal Fishing in the Carolinas,* and *American Aquarium Fishes.*

Cover Photos

Front cover: Kevin Webb (large photo, bottom right); K.A. Webb (top right, bottom left); Tony Terceira (middle right). Back cover: Aaron Norman (large photo, inset). Inside front cover: Aaron Norman. Inside back cover: Aaron Norman.

Photo Credits

K.A. Webb: 3, 11, 12 (top r, bottom l), 15, 16, 18, 19 (bottom), 22, 28 (top, bottom), 41 (top), 50, 66 (middle), 70 (middle, bottom), 72, 73, 77, 78, 82 (top l), 144. Ralf Britz: 62 (top, bottom), 67 (bottom), 79. Robert J. Goldstein: 20, 87, 88, 89, 90, 94, 98. Hiro Kishi: viii, 25, 43, 44, 52 (top, bottom), 53 (top), 56 (bottom), 59 (top), 61, 68, 74, 81, 82 (top r, bottom), 154. Aaron Norman: vii, 5, 8, 12 (top l), 57, 60 (top), 70 (top), 80, 111, 138, 142, 150. P.K.L. Ng: 41 (bottom), 59 (bottom), 60 (middle), 64, 65 (top), 67 (top), 76. Nonn Panitvong: 27, 55 (l, r), 66 (top), 75. H.H. Tan: 56 (top), 60 (bottom), 65 (bottom), 66 (bottom). Tony Terceira: 10, 14, 19 (top), 31, 36, 37, 38 (top, bottom), 39, 40, 42 (top, bottom), 53 (bottom), 58.

All inquiries should be addressed to:
Barron's Educational Series, Inc.
250 Wireless Boulevard
Hauppauge, New York 11788
www.barronseduc.com

ISBN-13: 978-0-7641-2728-1
ISBN-10: 0-7641-2728-4

Library of Congress Catalog Card No. 2004043721

Library of Congress Cataloging-in-Publication Data
Goldstein, Robert J. (Robert Jay), 1937–
    The betta handbook / Robert J. Goldstein.
        p.   cm.
    Includes bibliographical references (p.).
    ISBN 0-7641-2728-4
    1. Betta. I. Title.

 SF458.B4G64   2004
 639.3'77—dc22   2004043721

Printed in China
9 8 7 6 5 4

Contents

Preface and Acknowledgments

New species of *Betta* are constantly being discovered and named in scientific journals (sometimes in aquarium magazines), and offspring offered to aquarists through specialized clubs like the International Betta Congress (IBC) and the International Anabantoid Association (IAA) in the United States and other clubs overseas. In the last 20 years, Singaporean, Swiss, Dutch, and German scientists and British aquarists have introduced some 30 species to the hobby, and the total may approach 100 species when all areas are investigated.

The most notable investigators have been Maurice Kottelat, Kai-Erik Witte, P. K. L. Ng, Tan Heok Hui, Ralf Britz, Tan Swee Hee, Jurgen Schmidt, and Dieter Schaller. Allan and Barbara Brown pioneered the collection of species in peninsular Malaysia and Sarawak in the early 1980s, work that preceded the explosion of other collections and species descriptions from Singapore, Switzerland, and Germany. The Browns continue to bring in and breed new fishes, and make the offspring available to specialized *Betta* clubs. The aquarium writers Frank Schäfer, Horst Linke, H. J. Richter, H. Pinter, Jorge Vierke, and Walter Foersch described and named several new species in popular publications, and expanded our understanding of how these fishes breed and the natural environment where these fishes live. Scientists who describe new species often ignore the very ecological information so important to aquarists, although that is changing.

Several experts today are publishing photographs, information about the collecting sites, and breeding behaviors of new species in the popular commercial literature, in local club magazines, and on the web. Among the top contributors today are David Armitage, Mohd Noor Adnin, Nonn Panitvong, Yohan Fernando, Phil Dickman, Michael Schlueter, Jesper Thorup, Stefan van der Voort, Tony Pinto, Tony Terciera, Denis Yong, Tony Tejavej, Peter Chan, and Andrew Smith. Hobby workhorses who compile and distribute information from aquarists through editorships of the publications of specialized *Betta* clubs provide enormous help to us all (including scientists). We are all

Male Betta smaragdina *from the Korat Plateau.*

grateful for the contributions of people like Marleen Janson, Steve and Sallie Van Camp, Dr. Gene Lucas, Gilbert Limhengco, and Ralph Tran.

The seminal study that organized species of *Betta* into taxonomic groups is Witte and Schmidt (1992), who prepared a key to the genus and discussed the status of many unnamed forms. I've relied heavily on their analysis, and on Ralf Britz's new organization of *Betta* within the anabantoids. Drs. Tan and Ng at the National University of Singapore describe new species and revisit and revise the groups every year, and they have been most helpful to me in providing information for this book.

David Armitage, Tony Pinto, and Allan and Barbara Brown have made important suggestions for the reallocation of species into groups based on morphology and on direct experience of their habits, habitats, and distribution. Many others have provided information for each of the species.

Chapter One
Introduction

Labyrinth Fishes

Bettas are members of the bony fishes (class Teleostei), and the order Anabantoidei. The blue, pearl, kissing, and dwarf gouramies are well-known anabantoids. Less familiar anabantoids are the climbing perches and bushfish. We'll talk about them later in this book.

Anabantoids are commonly known as labyrinth fishes, referring to a specialized bone above the gill chamber. This structure starts out small in baby anabantoids, where it is called the epibranchial bone. As the fish grows and develops, so the bone folds and infolds upon itself. In the adult fish it usually has many convolutions that increase surface area. In the adult, this mature bone is called the suprabranchial bone. The suprabranchial becomes covered with epithelial tissue enriched with capillaries, much like your lungs or a fish's gills. The combination of the suprabranchial bone with its capillary-rich epithelium is called the

Betta enisae habitat at Empenang, Kapuas River, Borneo.

labyrinth, and it is a supplementary breathing organ. The complexity of the labyrinth structure is one feature used to classify families of fishes within the Anabantoidei. You might think that the more complex the labyrinth, the more modern the fish compared with its ancestors, but that isn't true. Bettas are modern anabantoids, yet their labyrinth is only a small straight tube. This simplification of the labyrinth seems to be derived from the convoluted condition in ancestral anabantoids.

The labyrinth helps anabantoids thrive where water is polluted from plant decay or so hot that it holds too little oxygen for most fishes (most pointedly, predators). Anabantoids can take a gulp of surface air (2,100 parts per million of oxygen) when there is little oxygen in the water. That's why they can live in water that may be as oxygen-poor as only 0–2 parts per million. Most fishes need 5–8 parts per million of oxygen in the surrounding water, so a little gulp of air goes a long way. (There are other fishes with this ability, some with an organ similar to a labyrinth, and others such as cat-fishes that have a capillary-rich intestine that can also act as a lung.) And it isn't only getting oxygen that's important, but also eliminating (exhaling) carbon dioxide. When fish are packed too tightly or too long, it isn't the lack of oxygen that eventually kills them, but the buildup of carbon dioxide, which, at high concentrations, cause fish (and people) to stop breathing.

Labyrinth fishes can be shipped with barely enough water to keep them wet, plus air space in the container. That air space provides sufficient oxygen for the trip and, equally important, a space into which carbon dioxide can diffuse out of the water. This independence from a large volume of water (as an oxygen source) enables us to keep anabantoids in small confined spaces and even polluted water, as long as air is above. Bettas need little space, eat anything and never very much, should have the occasional water change, and thrive under conditions that other beginners' fishes, such as angelfish and neon tetras, would not survive.

The Siamese fighting fish is one of the first fish you see in a pet store and one of the first you purchase. But do you know where it comes from, how it lives, and how to get it to reproduce? And do you know how to raise the babies? That's what this book is about and, more than that, we'll also talk about all the other members of this intriguing genus.

Siamese Fighting Fish

Siamese fighting fish come from Thailand and nearby lands of Southeast Asia. Because of their popularity, they have been introduced everywhere. Today they even occur as breeding populations in Florida and Brazil, but you can't blame the fish. People breed them for fun or profit and throw away the excess, often into nearby streams and lakes that have never seen an anabantoid. These released fish are usually gobbled up by native predators, but in some parts of the world they have survived and thrived.

Breeders of decorative and of fighting strains from Thailand to Texas select the best offspring for future breeding. They look for long finnage, perhaps large bodies, and almost always unusual colors. Southeast Asian breeders care about fighting ability. How does it work? To know the fish, imagine that you are in the fighting fish market in downtown Bangkok, where vendors hawk wares from racks of jars containing strikingly beautiful or menacing large-bodied bettas. Nearby a group of men crowd around a small table on which there is a small glass tank. People bring strong fish to these fights, and money to back up their champions.

To set up a fight, two robust males are placed in a small jar, and money is placed on the table in favor of one fish or the other. In China to the far north, the cold-tolerant paradise fish (*Macropodus opercularis*)

Short-fin plakat.

is used in much the same way, although fighting paradise fishes is not as popular. Fighting strains of *Betta splendens* have only recently been imported into the United States in response to demand from new Southeast Asian immigrants from Vietnam and Thailand, but fighting strains of paradise fish have not been imported, despite the much larger Chinese community.

Fighting

It isn't their fault! Fighting fish do not fight in nature, or at least not very hard. Like many other species, the males of the Siamese fighting fish are normally territorial, and defend those territories from competitor males. Chase away the competitor, and everyone is happy. To get a fighting fish to fight, breeders do two things.

First, they selectively breed champions. What makes a champion? Large size, big head, and powerful jaws all help, but as in humans, being a champion is more than physical strength. It has a lot to do with heart or the willingness to keep going despite adversity and pain. Champion fighting fish are all of this—powerful in body and jaw, and relentless in aggressiveness.

Also like professional fighters, native ability isn't enough, but must be supplemented with training. Capture a wild male or even grow a domestically bred male, and it isn't aggressive enough to be a champion. It must be trained.

Fighting fish are trained by removing males from a group and placing each in a small jar shielded (with paper or cardboard) so each cannot see the others. After a month, each male's world (and territory) consists of that small prison that may be no more than 1 quart (1 L) or 1 gallon (4 L) area. When two males with this experience are taken from their jars and placed together, they both defend and protect "their" territory, first by aggressive threat displays (flared fins and gill covers) and then by biting if the competitor does not flee. Because both are confined and neither can flee, a fight is inevitable.

This training of killers by confining them and selecting for fish with courage, aggressiveness, big jaws, and robust bodies results in fishes born and bred for fighting. They are not pretty, but they are tough. This sport and all it takes is foreign to Americans, but the Thai people probably think our prisons are inhumane, considering we treat prisoners like they treat fish.

Several species of fighting fish and their hybrids are now used in Thai fights. The recent large immigration of Asians to the United States has also created a demand for fighting plakat, and those are now being imported to this country. Because a fish is used to fight only one time, there is a large demand.

After that one fight, the fish is retired, and its cohorts (brothers from the same batch) used for further bouts, also just one time for each fish. Losers and their cohorts are not used for further breeding. It is the cohorts of winning fish that are bred to produce a new generation of fighters.

The Chinese use paradise fish (*Macropodus opercularis*) for fighting, in the same way the Thai use *Betta splendens*. However, competitive bouts between paradise fish have never been popularized here by Chinese-Americans.

Names

The Thai name for Siamese fighting fish is Plakat Thai. Wild fish are called Plakat Thung, referring to plakat from swamps. Domestic fighting fish are called Plakat Lukmoh, with Lukmoh referring to the clay pots used for breeding. As you might expect, fish bred for fighting will fight for hours, whereas fish bred for show might quit after 10 minutes. Plakat Cheen fish are those bred for coloration, whether they have a satin sheen to the body or fancy dress (fins or coloration). "Cheen" refers to the Chinese culture, whose fancy silk robes come to mind when viewing these red, green, blue, or white beauties.

History

The fighting fish was imported into France from Siam (today's Thailand) in 1874. Some 19 years later, in 1893, the French aquarist Jeunet described how it spawned. It was then rapidly distributed throughout Europe. During this period the fish was erroneously called *Betta pugnax*, because that was the only valid species in the scientific literature at the time, and this fish was certainly *Betta*. In America, the ichthyologist C. Tate Regan saw preserved specimens of fighting fish, recognized that this fish was not the

Long-fin red betta.

same as preserved *Betta pugnax*, and described it as a new species, which he named *Betta splendens*.

In 1910, live specimens were exported to the United States, where they were an instant hit with aquarists. In 1927, the first white fish imported to the United States was named *Betta cambodia*, but it was soon recognized as just a color variant of *Betta splendens*.

Fighting never became popular in the United States or Europe until recently, but fighting always was and to this day is popular in Thailand, with more species and even hybrids entering the sport. Today's fighting species include *Betta splendens, B. smaragdina, B. imbellis, B. prima*, and *B. pi*.

Fighting aside, *Betta splendens* has become one of the world's most popular aquarium fishes. Long-finned and spectacularly colored males are some of the most hardy, beautiful, and inexpensive aquarium fishes available. Males are usually kept in small bowls or jars because their delicate elongated fins are easily torn in a community tank, because they often hide from aggressive fish in big tanks, and because they sometimes are aggressive toward smaller fishes. Besides, it's hard to see them in all their glory unless you can see them close up. Beginners and even professional breeders usually display the males in individual containers of 1 gallon (4 L) or even smaller. If you place a mirror against the tank, the male will react with a spectacular display of flaring gill plates, threatening undulations and charges, and magnificently stretched fins as the male threatens that image of a competitor in the mirror by appearing larger than he really is. Many animals do the same thing with whatever they have. Cats puff up by erecting their hairs.

Toads swallow air. Birds erect their feathers. Humans wear feathers or helmets with spikes on their heads, and try to look larger by wearing oversized shirts and shoes.

Females are smarter, recognizing that if you increase visibility, you increase your vulnerability to predators. The dull-colored, short-fin female bettas are not as pretty as aquarium fishes, and are less in demand. They are peaceful community tank fishes that get along with other species and with each other. Female birds are also often dull colored. Did you ever wonder why women outnumber men?

Siamese fighting fish are excellent beginner fish, requiring no special foods, needing no special warm temperatures nor quality of water, and eating anything offered, despite their nature as carnivorous fishes that, in the wild, eat mostly insects. They do well at room temperatures, but tolerate high temperatures that would drive all the life-sustaining oxygen out of the water and kill other fishes. They are seldom affected by cold temperatures that would decimate tetras or angelfish. They are exceptionally temperature tolerant for tropical fish. When it's hot, they gulp air and oxygen from the surface, and when it's cold, they simply slow down and become lethargic.

Chapter Two

Characteristics of the Genus

The first bettas imported from Asia for the aquarium trade were long-fin *Betta splendens*. The more common, fighting, short-fin plakat popular in Thailand was unknown here. The long-fin variety (a cull, or throwaway, if you are a fighting advocate) was highly regarded in a western world that cared only about beauty and compatibility and not fighting. Long-fin bettas were available in shades of blue, green, and red. The next variety imported was the Cambodia *Betta splendens* with colored fins (shades of green, blue, and red) on a white body.

Betta names are a mix of common names, shorthand, genetic terms, and spurious names. Common names might be veil tail or double tail and their shorthand (for advertising or popular publications) might be VT or DT. Genetic terms for mutations refer to the gene (or gene cluster), where the plus sign (+) refers to the most common allele (the wild type), a capital letter refers to an allele dominant to the wild-type gene, and a lower-case letter refers to an allele recessive to the wild-type, or common, allele. Spurious names are those hawked by sellers of fish that may not meet show standards for accepted types, and are invented to generate sales of "something new."

Because almost all breeding today consists of crosses among sports (variants) of varying dominance relationships and with interactions among nonalleles affecting the same trait, and because wild-type genes for desirable traits have almost disappeared from breeding stock in the aquarium hobby, the plus sign (+) for wild type, in my opinion, has no value in today's breeding analyses, and furthermore obscures relationships among and between the traits we wish to understand.

Today many varieties of *Betta splendens* are recognized (sanctioned) by the International Betta Congress (IBC) and other groups that breed show bettas. The varieties are based on color, finnage, pigment, guanine depositions, fin ray number, and fin shape. Recognized classes and judging standards are complex, and certification as a judge requires considerable study and an apprenticeship.

Fringe-fin plakat.

A novice who doesn't know the accepted names will be overwhelmed by the commercial names (pretending to be unique forms) used by Internet vendors. Beware any name used only by one vendor, because it may be hyperbole. When vendors use the same name (e.g., Cambodia, double tail, butterfly), you know what they mean, but a unique name often masks an effort to sell novices the culls, or throwaways, that fail to meet standards of a recognized class or allelic type.

Fin Types

Dr. Gene Lucas summarized fin **shapes** as round (wild type), half-moon (shovel shaped), spade tailed or pin tailed (lancet shaped), veil tail or long fin (flowing and extended), delta (triangular with a vertical end), and ribbon (elongated flowing). Veil tail or long fin is dominant to wild type (+) and the gene symbol is *P*

from the German *prachtig*. Sellers sometimes advertise veil tail as VT, long fin as LF, and half-moon as HM, but these are shorthand for the phenotype (what they look like) and should not be confused with their genotype. It's good practice to indicate *genotypes* in *italics*.

Fins are also specially named if there is an **increase in the number of rays**. A common mutation is doubling or tripling of the rays. When this happens, the fish is classified as a double tail. The clusters of increased rays above and below the centerline of the tail often look like separate bundles, as if the number of tails has doubled when, in fact, the number of rays has doubled. Double tails also have increased rays in the dorsal and anal fins (at least), but here the rays appear in a continuous row. Double tail usually crowds the rays, so the fin takes up no more space on the body than a normal fin. A variant of double tail has the rays uncrowded, the fin arising from a larger basal area on the fish. The double tail (dt) trait is recessive to the wild type (+ or DT), so you must ask clarification when a seller offers a "DT" betta—that is, is he using DT as shorthand for double tail or as its genotype? If the latter, then the fish may have normal-looking finnage, because the trait is recessive (and genetically should be called dt).

Fins can also be classified by the **extent of rays** beyond to the margin of the fin membrane. When rays extend (normally) to the edge of the membrane, the fins are smooth

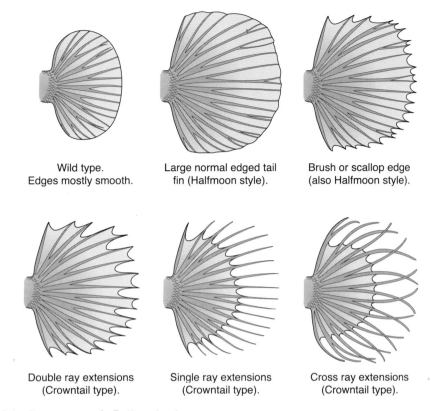

| Wild type. Edges mostly smooth. | Large normal edged tail fin (Halfmoon style). | Brush or scallop edge (also Halfmoon style). |
| Double ray extensions (Crowntail type). | Single ray extensions (Crowntail type). | Cross ray extensions (Crowntail type). |

Major finnage types in Betta splendens.

edged. If they extend a bit beyond the membrane and seem to carry the membrane with them, the fins are called brush or scalloped. In this case, the membrane between the rays appears to be indented or to have grown less than the more-vigorous fin rays. A variant of scalloped that occurs with double tails is with the indentations alternating between deep and shallow. Finally, there is the crown tail variant, where the rays extend far beyond the membrane and look like filamentous strands on the fin. Crown tails occur with rays parallel or crossed. We think smooth edged is dominant (+) to protruding rays (p).

What's wrong with this analysis? Let me count the ways! First, we don't have separate symbols for doubling versus tripling of fin rays, even though they must be separate genes or, more likely, *a duplication of the triplet sequence on the DNA*. Replications are repeats of genetic sequences (A,T,T,G...) that can manifest as (1) no effect, (2) an increase in a structure or a color density or the production of any other chemical, or (3) a nonviable or lethal effect, whereby the fish dies or can't reproduce to pass its genes to the next generation. We may in fact have a range of double-tail mutations, which might then be indicated as dt-1, dt-2, dt-3, and so on.

Second, we don't have reproducible data on the results of crossing extent-of-rays strains, such as brush with crown tail. Will there be dominance or incomplete dominance, or are they not alleles nor otherwise interact? Will the offspring inherit both types of genes, and what will that look like? Will the genes show dominance or incomplete dominance, or will they mask each other by wild type? Is either gene sex-linked or sex limited, and is this true of all strains showing this trait or has the mutation occurred more than once in different lines?

Double-tail green betta.

Without documentation of all offspring of crosses through several generations, we can't know how many genes are responsible, which genes are alleles, which genes are not alleles but interact, and which genes are not alleles and do not interact. Without these answers, there is no basis for assuming a single gene or multiple genes or any other interaction. That is why breeders use line breeding to refine their strains. All you need to know is that relentless culling will fix the strain.

Iridescence and Opaqueness

Bettas eliminate wastes from the gills and kidneys, but they also deposit some wastes in the skin, eyes, and fins. These compounds are called guanines, nontoxic polymers of ammonia. They may be deposited as crystalline arrays in the epidermis or as random granules in the underlying dermis. If they are layered as crystals, they refract light and generate an iridescent sheen. When crystalline guanine is deposited in epidermal cells, those cells are then called iridocytes.

Wild bettas have almost all their iridocytes in the upper body and fins. Domesticated bettas are selectively bred to increase the distribution of iridocytes even onto the head. The thickness and depth of the crystals affects whether a fish is green or blue (a simple wavelength difference), and variation in green and blue is affected by density of crystal packing and by any underlying melanin (black) pigments.

The term "spread iridescence" is when iridescent scales occur everywhere (all over the head, body, and fins), rather than just on the body exclusive of the head. The term is sometimes attached to other descriptors. The same condition is sometimes called "extended iridescence."

The mutant called "opaque" has waste guanine deposited in granules. These granules don't produce iridescence because they cannot refract light (which requires a crystalline arrangement). The guanine makes these fish milky or matt. The guanine deposits are harmless in the body, but if they extend to the eyes they can cause blindness. Opaque bettas are matt or flat and readily distinguished from Cambodia bettas, which may glow or glisten.

Colors

The colors green and blue in bettas and many other fish are not caused by pigments any more than the colors of the ocean or the sky. In fishes, they are manifestations of light refracted by guanine crystals in the epidermis after bouncing off dermal layers containing melanin. Japanese studies of damselfish (*Chrysiptera cyanea*) showed how they rapidly change from violet to blue or green because of motile iridophores that rapidly change their distance from underlying melano-

Blue crowntail betta.

phores and each other. The intensity and shade of the green, blue, or violet also depends on whether melanosomes are expanded or contracted. The distance of the iridophore's guanine crystals from one another and from the dispersed or contracted melanophores changes the refraction of light. When light is refracted to emit at a wavelength of 532 nanometers, the fish appears green, but when the wavelength shifts to 485 nm, the fish becomes blue (*Oshima et al., 1985; Fujii and Oshima, 1986; Kasukawa et al., 1986*). At least in damselfish, sudden hormone release rapidly determines the color of the moment. It's likely that this system is the same in bettas, where color is fixed because the iridophores are not motile, but stuck in crystalline arrays, and melanosome dispersal and contraction play a minor role. In bettas, green, blue, and steel blue are traits that can be predicted as the result

Female cornflower blue betta.

Half-moon tail blue betta.

of two interacting genes showing incomplete dominance (blending). These genes control the distance and orientation of guanine crystals in relation to the underlying melanin deposits.

Incomplete dominance is a blending of the effects of two alleles. An IBC document explains what happens when you cross a green betta (GG) with a steel blue betta (BlBl).

The color of the offspring (BlG) is cornflower blue, a mix of steel blue (Bl) and green (G). That's why show rules place cornflower blue (mixed), green (pure), and steel blue (pure) in different categories.

		G	G (green male)
(steel	Bl	GBl	GBl
blue			
female)	Bl	GBl	GBl

All the offspring are cornflower blue phenotypes, carrying genes for blue and green (genotype GBl). An intermediate wavelength is emitted, probably because the crystalline guanine layers are neither deep nor shallow, but intermediate in depth. Suppose you want pure steel blue or green breeding stock but have only cornflower blue bettas? Simply cross a cornflower blue brother to its cornflower blue sister, and you can regenerate the pure parental phenotypes.

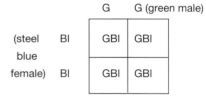

Steel blue crowntail betta.

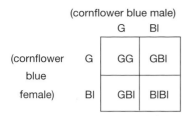

		(cornflower blue male)	
		G	Bl
(cornflower	G	GG	GBl
blue			
female)	Bl	GBl	BlBl

The offspring should be about 25 percent green (GG), 25 percent pure or steel blue (BlBl), and 50 percent cornflower blue (GBl).

Pigments

There's more to betta colors than meets the eye. The same colors in different strains of bettas may be caused by different mutations. In addition, any one pigment may take on more than one color.

Two (or ten) red strains (or any other color strain) may have different origins in genes from different locations on the DNA, so these genes are not alleles. If they were, you would expect either dominance or blending, but if they are not alleles, then a cross should produce wild types. Linebreeding will tell you in the first generation whether two reds are caused by different genes or the same gene.

Pigments are usually inside chromatophores in the dermis (the inner layer, or "sub-skin") and in the eyes. Most chromatophores are in cells called melanocytes. Melanocytes make brown or black (and sometimes yellow) melanin pigment. They also expand (the fish darkens) and con-

tract (the fish lightens). A second kind of chromatophore is the xanthophore, containing yellow xanthins derived from oils and other colored substances (perhaps yellow, orange, or red). A third chromatophore is the erythrophore, containing red (or blue, black, or purple) pigments called pterins and related substances. These three kinds of chromatophores can produce many pigments in different hues and intensities. There can be various combinations of pigments and chromatophores (black can result from melanin or pterin or can even mask or cover up a half dozen other pigments). It is the combination of pigment types, sometimes their incomplete development, and often their interactions that produce betta colors. Furthermore, any one pigment carrier (erythrophore, melanophore, xanthophore) may contain several kinds of pigments. That isn't surprising considering that all these carriers ("-phores") arise from the same embryonic tissue and are named for their most common pigment, rather than for any substantial differences.

Melanin

The most common pigment is melanin, and it usually makes the fish black or brown. A fish deficient in melanin is lighter, and extremely light fish without melanin are called xanthic. You may have seen xanthic minnows, lighter fish that stand out from the school (and are easy pickings for predators). Xanthic fish are generally called "semialbinos." A complete lack of melanin is albinism. Albinos are

Black bicolor show betta.

CH₂-CH-COOH ... (chemical structures)

Tyrosine

3,4-Dihydroxydiphenyl-
alanine (DOPA)

Dopa quinone

5,6-Dihydroxydihydro-
indole-α-carboxylic
acid

Dopa chrome

5,6-Dihydroxyindole

Indole 5,6-quinone

Dopa melanin

Chemical steps in the formation of melanin from tyrosine.

xanthic fish that lack pigment in the eyes, so they have poor vision in bright daylight. They are the easiest of all pickings for predators, and that's why so few survive in the wild.

Melanin is manufactured in the body from the amino acid alanine. Animals use alanine for proteins and other substances. By tagging on a phenyl group (a phenyl is a common type of ring structure), the amino acid becomes phenylalanine. It, too, is used as a component of proteins, but it has many additional uses.

Chemical reactions in the body don't just happen, or we'd all melt. These reactions are controlled by a class of enabling proteins called enzymes. Now bear with me and I'll explain how this relates to melanin.

Enzymes called mixed-function oxidases convert phenylalanine to hydroxyphenylalanine (because of the addition of an –OH, or "hydroxy," group). This hydroxyphenylalanine is known by its nickname, tyrosine.

Tyrosine is one of the most important chemicals in the body. Adding a second hydroxy group, it becomes dihydroxyphenylalanine, abbreviated DOPA. Your doctor can inject DOPA to ameliorate the trembling of Parkinson's disease. The conversion of tyrosine to DOPA is under the control of another enzyme called tyrosinase. People who lack tyrosinase in the brain may get Parkinson's symptoms, and those who lack tyrosinase in the dermis and sometimes the eyes may become xanthic or even albino.

We're not done. Inside the melanocyte, the DOPA ring is altered into a more complex quinone ring, again using a specific enzyme to facilitate the reaction. DOPA is colorless. Quinones are often colored. The quinone derived from DOPA is called DOPA quinone, and it is red. Is that a way to get red fish? Probably not in bettas. DOPA quinone is chemically unstable and loses an important acidic side chain known as the –COOH, or carboxyl, group. No enzyme is needed. The result of spontaneous decarboxylation (loss of the –COOH) is a new, colored substance called indole quinone.

Indole quinone combines with itself over and over in a process called polymerization to form the pigment melanin. Melanin combines with a protein, and that protein is the melanoprotein. It is melanoproteins we see in black and brown fish.

Why black or brown? Melanin can be oxidized or reduced. When it's in the oxidized configuration (=O), melanin appears black, and when it is in the reduced configuration (–OH), it appears brown.

Black or Melano

The black betta types are called smoky, charcoal, impure (glistening), and pure matt black (melano). As we've seen in melanin formation, more melanin may not make the fish blacker if the melanin is in the reduced (–OH) state. We need to oxidize melanin for maximum blackness. The key to getting black might be dietary or even temperature related, as in Siamese cats.

Short-fin, steel, blue-black betta.

The smoky black betta is dark gray. Smoky breeds true and is a good strain to use for line breeding to increase oxidized melanin, but not to get a melano (pure black).

The blackest mutation unfortunately results in females that produce nonviable eggs that don't develop normally and yield no fry. To keep black going, we breed the black melano male to a steel (pure) blue female. Breeding the offspring to each other yields pure black melano males that can again be bred to steel blue females to maintain the strain. When black males are bred to cornflower blue females, those blacks develop some iridescence that fails to meet the IBC's goal of a matt black fish without iridescence or "shine." Blackness can be darkened if red is included in the genotype, but any appearance of red in fins is a fault, as is any appearance of yellow

Black bicolor betta.

spots. The ultimate goal is a fertile melano strain that does not depend on outcrosses to keep going. We're not there yet.

Why can't we get a strain of pure black (and fertile) bettas? We can speculate that putting so much DOPA into melanin deprives the fish of DOPA for thyroid function, brain function, and hormones and neurotransmitters. DOPA hooked onto iodine creates diiodotyrosine (also called thyroxin). Some DOPA is converted to norepinephrine and then to epinephrine. Epinephrine and thyroxin are needed for controlling the concentration of sugars in the gut, blood, and cells. Failure of DOPA to make neurotransmitters, thyroxin, and epinephrine is lethal.

Most betta breeders consider the gene for black to be recessive to wild type, and symbolize it as *m* for

melano. It's also been proposed that xanthism, which is recessive, be called "blond" and symbolized as *b*. However, "xanthic" is an established term in fisheries, and is a deficiency of black in the body but not the eyes. The melano versus blond represents alleles rather than separate genes.

There is another complication. If we cross a black to a charcoal, we get wild type. The mutations are therefore in different genes. Until we know all the genes for black, smoky, charcoal, and blond, we cannot establish genetic symbols and assume relationships.

Finally, we've seen that melanin formation requires several different enzymes. Because a gene codes for a single enzyme, the color black depends on several genes. Therefore, a single symbol indicating a single black gene is incorrect and will only lead to further confusion.

Xanthic, Albino, and Semialbino

A lack of tyrosinase activity causes albinism, the absence of melanin. Other pigments in albinos, including reds and yellows, remain, or there may be no other colors. Partial albinism occurs when tyrosinase occurs in some tissues but not others, or the melanophores cannot expand. Partial albinism is called xanthism. Xanthic fish are white or colorless with normal, dark pigment in the eyes. Xanthic color types range from white to yellow. The fish may be genetically competent to make melanin (it has the tyrosinase genes), but the enzyme is produced only in the eyes and not in the skin. How can this be?

It isn't complicated. Why do we make insulin in the pancreas and not everywhere? Why do skin cells make hair follicles, but liver cells don't? It is because the *controller* regions of the genes in the nucleus of the cell direct the cell's machinery to make one kind of protein and not another. Although all cells have the same DNA, the controller regions of DNA for each kind of tissue (skin, pancreas, liver) instruct that cell to make some products in that tissue but not in others.

Semialbinos, or xanthics, are widespread, and we see them in pet stores as fixed yellows or strains lacking melanin everywhere but the eyes. If the eyes are black, it's because melanin is still made there. If the eyes are red, it's because there is no melanin there to protect them from bright light, and we see the eye's blood vessels. An albino has red eyes and a body without melanin.

Semialbinos may be caused by a lost or nonfunctioning single gene that codes for tyrosinase, so it is not produced in the body, but continues to be produced in the eyes. Or semialbinos could be deficient in one of the other genes used in melanin formation. Or they could be produced from an entirely different mutation unrelated to melanin, one that causes the melanophores to be permanently contracted.

Xanthic fish with crystalline guanine iridescence are sometimes called golds or platinums.

Black and xanthic bettas result from the distribution and concentration of oxidized melanin, tyrosinase, expanded melanocytes, or a combination of factors.

What then is the range of colors in bettas resulting from melanin? Colors range from black, to brown, to yellow, to white, and even to Cambodia, although Cambodia is a special case.

Cambodia, Opaque, and Pastel

Cambodia is a semialbino, or xanthic, type, where the loss of melanin is limited to the dermis of the body. Activity of tyrosinase (and production of melanin) is normal in eyes. Although all the cells have the same DNA and the tyrosinase gene isn't missing, its controller has shut down tyrosinase production in the body but not in the eyes.

There may be guanine crystals in Cambodia betta fins that make them iridescent green or blue, or there may be red pterins turned on by controller regions in the fins (but not the body). We generally talk about Cambodia being inherited as a single gene recessive trait denoted *c*. That may be true or not. The mutation may affect the production of tyrosinase in trunk tissues only. Many Cambodia bettas have yellow bodies, indicating xanthin pigments in the dermis, unrelated to albinism, but that has nothing to do with melanin.

Pastel and Opaque

The strains of bettas called *opaque* are semialbinos with guanine

Half-moon Cambodia plakat.

particles instead of crystals in the epidermis. If the fish has a blue or green iridescence, that is the result of crystalline guanine on the trunk, and it is called a *pastel.* How we get a blue or green sheen without underlying dermal melanin is not yet understood.

Reverse Cambodia

Some new strains have dark bodies and yellow fins, and breed true. The yellow in the fins is either a xanthin or, as Dr. Gene Lucas has suggested, an interruption in the pterin pathway that Lucas calls "nonred" because the final red color of this pathway is not attained. There are reverse Cambodia bettas with black or brown bodies and yellow fins, and fish with iridescent blue or green bodies and yellow fins. The fin and body pigments and deposits of crystalline guanine are inherited separately on different genes, or are

turned on and off in body and fins by different DNA controllers in different tissues.

Cellophane

Cambodia bettas may lose IBC show points for overwashes of iridescence on the body, yet breeders continue to flout the rule and produce new, attractive strains. One variant is *cellophane*, in which all the black (melanin), red (pterin), and blue and green (refraction) colors are missing from the fins, which have only a yellow wash perhaps caused by a xanthins or carotenoids. Cellophanes retain the black eye, so they are not albinos.

Orange

The *orange* betta originated from a cross between a standard Cambodia and an opaque white Cambodia with red fins. The offspring had mostly opaque (guanine particles)

Red cellophane fan-tail.

bodies and red fins or pastel (crystalline guanine) bodies and red fins, but there were also just a few yellow (xanthic) and cellophane bettas. The smallest cellophanes were saved (usually runts are discarded), and though they grew slowly, they eventually became a deep yellow or even reddish yellow everywhere on the body and fins. These became the original *orange* stock. Gilbert Limhengco, who developed this strain, believes the orange color is derived from the red Cambodia pigment. If that's true, then the change is probably from a single red pterin to a mix of deep yellowish orange pterins, an interruption in the pterin pathway, or an extra DNA region for this pigment.

Marble and Pied

The erratic distribution of blues or greens on a predominantly Cambodia body is called *marble*. When this erratic distribution includes partially unpigmented fins, the fish is called *pied*, although some use the terms interchangeably. There are mostly blue and green marbles and mostly blue pieds. This implies that marble may be the erratic distribution of melanin (or of expanded melanocytes) in the dermis that affects blue or green colors produced from

Long-fin orange male.

Pied blue, spawning.

epidermal guanine crystals. Marbles may have many patterns in a single strain. Marbles occasionally produce an albino, but so far nobody has fixed an albino strain.

Red Pigments
Red can be produced from carotenoid or from pterin pigments, probably not from interrupted melanin formation. The condition of red pigment on the body, the head, and the fins is called *extended red*. The term has also been used for deep wine red fish that combine red pterins with black melanins to produce a deep shade of red. We'll discuss carotenoids and pterins separately.

Carotenoids
Carotenoids are polymers of simple molecules called terpenes. Terpenes are carbon chains with alternating double bonds ($-C=C-C=C-$) and methyls ($-CH_3$). Terpenes are important provitamins, toxins, pigments, and medicines. Many physiologically reactive substances in corals and marine algae are terpenes that have anticancer and anti-AIDS activity.

The most important terpene polymers are the carotenoids. Beta-carotene, a provitamin, converts to the most common form of vitamin A. vitamin A helps enzymes to function. Without the vitamin, the enzyme doesn't work. There are other carotenes (alpha, gamma) and other forms of vitamin A. Carotenoids are also important for vision pigments.

Many carotenoids are yellow, orange, or red. Breeders select bettas that can concentrate carotenoids and become yellow or orange fish. Dietary supplements are needed to maintain the coloration derived from carotenoids. Yellow in fishes may also be caused by xanthophores, and those do not require dietary supplies. The most common dietary carotenoid is astaxanthin, a pigment found in high concentrations in *Spirulina*, a blue-green alga that is the most common astaxanthin source in fish foods. Another source is paprika.

Yellow
Yellow colors are possible through the melanin pathway for pigments and neurotransmitters, the xanthin

pathways for carotenoids like astaxanthin and beta-carotene, or the pterin pathways for vitamins like folic acid. In any strain, it may be caused by one or several mutations. Not all yellows are from carotenoids, nor are they all in xanthophores, nor are all yellows from one source. It is possible to have a Cambodia derived from carotenoids in xanthophores (particularly the yellowish Cambodias) or other causes (incomplete melanin formation or even a pterin origin). When crossing yellow (or orange or red) fish from two different lines that happen to look alike, it is common to get wild-type offspring, indicating that the colors were caused by different genes.

Pterins

Red pigment can result from interrupted melanin formation ending with DOPA-quinone, but the substance is unstable, so that seems an unlikely cause of red in bettas. Another kind of red can result from the xanthin pathway. Red has been confirmed to be caused by pterin pigments in platys, swordtails, and fruit flies, and seems to also be one cause of red in bettas.

Pterins are made of chemicals called pteridines. These pteridines are almost identical to guanine. Guanine in the betta skin is a waste product of nitrogen metabolism. Katherine Royal, a student of Dr. Gene Lucas, showed in the 1970s that red in *Betta splendens* is caused

Chemical pterin ring structure and the specific structure of xanthopterin.

Pterin

Xanthopterin
(2-amino-4,6-dihydroxy pteridine)

by both pterin pigments (in pterinosomes) and carotenoid pigments. Royal determined that at least two mutations produce several different strains of red betta. These strains differ in the presence or absence of pterins and the carotenoid astaxanthin, and their concentrations when either or both pigments are present.

Pterins work with folic acid, an important B vitamin. Folic acid regulates the enzyme xanthine oxidase, used in the metabolism of uric acid (related to ammonia, urea, and guanine). Bettas don't need all those pteridines for good health, and store the excess red chemical in pterinosomes in the dermis. So we see a repeat of the guanine story (that leads to iridescence or opacity), this time leading to red fish.

Overview

The primordial pigment cell in fish development is derived from an embryonic stem cell that can develop into any kind of pigment cell.

Male **Betta foerschi.**

Melanophores are famous for containing the pigment melanin, but melanin can be yellow, brown, or black. Further, those same melanophores might also carry carotenoids. Pterinosomes are formed during xanthophore differentiation in the embryo. Xanthophores can contain xanthins (yellow or orange pigments), carotenoids (yellow, orange, or red pigments), pterins (red, yellow, black, blue, or orange pigments), or a combination of pigments. Separate erythrophores might contain other red, yellow, or black pigments. None of these colors results from a single gene. A pigment is produced by a pathway of several enzymes (each built from DNA to nuclear RNA to cytoplasmic RNA) that carry a molecule through a pathway of changes until that pigment results (or it stops at an intermediate step). These pathways can all result in a changed color if they lack a single enzyme in a series (the color depending on which enzyme in which series), or, more likely, if they have a controller region

of a gene that is switched off when it should be switched on, and vice versa. Finally, domestic betta strains are the result of combinations of mutations in some or all these pathways. That is why simple one and two gene models usually fail to predict the outcomes of crosses.

Today we have tools to transfer genes between species. We can locate genes that were turned off in the past and switch them back on. The variations and colors of domestic bettas will be far different 20 years from now.

We know little about the genetic basis of most strains. Which phenotypes are caused by interactions among different parts of the DNA rather than alleles? Which mutations differ by a single amino acid, a single nucleotide base pair, or extended strand of DNA? Which phenotypes result from promotor or controller regions of a gene responding to the chemistry of a specific tissue so that the mutation appears in some tissues (fins, eyes, body) but not others?

Chapter Three
Bubblenesting Bettas

Some *Betta* species are widespread, ranging throughout Indochina and through the Malay Peninsula, or across the Strait of Melaka (a.k.a. Molucca or Malacca) into the Greater Sunda Islands of Sumatra and Java. Others have restricted distributions in single river systems on just one island, and have ranges that do not overlap (allopatric) with those of related species. For more extensive information on the subject of betta zoogeography (where bettas have historically lived and bred), refer to Chapter 7 of this book. When several *Betta* species occur together (sympatric) in the same stream, they are commonly members of different groups, or have different ecological niches (shoreline versus open water, leaf litter versus vegetation, different types of vegetation, different prey, different spawning seasons). This niche specialization means that they share the same water body without interfering with one another. Many habitats are flowing or stagnant at different seasons. Mouthbrooders may occur in the same streams as bubblenesters. Generalizations beg for exceptions, and we often find them in *Betta*.

Bubblenester Basics

Betta species are seldom restricted to specific habitats (the *coccina* and *waseri* groups and the hard water–requiring *B. simplex* being exceptions). When we read that a species occurs in a specific habitat, it may be based on a few reports where the fish was common. These habitat descriptions provide guidance, but are not the only way to keep a species in captivity. A species may be common in one kind of habitat not because that habitat is required, but because that habitat can be tolerated, whereas it is intolerable to competitors or predators.

Bubblenesters usually live in stagnant or still habitats, such as lakes, ponds, and ditches, river backwaters, and overflow pools in floodplains. The antibacterial mucus of the bubbles defining the nest provides eggs and prolarvae protection from microbes, and the sticky bubbles support eggs and fry near the surface film. The early larvae do not yet have gills or labyrinth, and oxygen (richest at the surface film) is absorbed

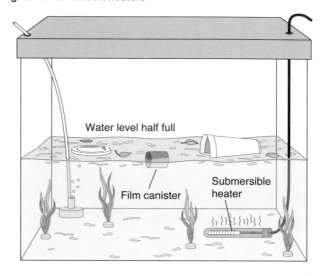

Breeding Tanks for Bubblenesters

- Fish Size → Tank Size
  - 1-3"   5-10 gal.
  - >3"   20 gal.

- Tank Cover   Yes

- Lighting   Yes

- Surface Structures
  - Half of a plastic cup
  - Plastic lid (coffee can top OK)
  - Dead tree leaves
  - Plastic film canister

- Bottom Structures
  - Not applicable

- Filtration
  - Sponge filter (slow)

- Temperature   74°-84°
  - heater(submersible)
- pH   4.5-7.2
  - (adjust with dead leaves, peat)
- Vegetation   Surface and bottom
- Gravel   Not needed

Water level half full

Film canister

Submersible heater

How to set up a breeding tank for bubblenesters.

directly through the body. The bubblenesters on average range from the size of *Betta splendens* (3 inch [7.5 cm]) to half that in the *coccina* group, whereas the mouthbrooders may grow considerably larger.

You can easily breed any bubblenester in 2–10 gallon (6–38 L) tanks. Larger tanks should be partially filled to keep the parents close to each other, the fry close to the surface, and the food concentrated where the fry can easily find it. Abundant vegetation (twigs, leaves, and Java moss) will protect females from impatient or aggressive males. Wild bettas, as a group, are not aggressive. This isn't surprising, because wild bettas have no baggage of being linebred for

fighting. In addition, fighting is a learned behavior. An ideal breeding tank would be a 20 gallon (76 L) tank filled to just 6 inches (15 cm) for spawning. After the fry become free-swimming, tanks are gradually filled to accommodate growth.

Distinct groups of *Betta* species sometimes have different ideal conditions. Members of the *splendens* group do best in neutral water of moderate calcium-magnesium hardness. Members of the *coccina* and *waseri* groups do best in soft, acidic, deeply stained water. Soft water can be rain running off the roof, prepared from deionization cartridges or reverse osmosis units, or purchased in gallon jugs from your local supermarket. See pages 24 and 35 for tips on preparing this specialized water.

Philippine Java moss (*Vesicularia dubyana*), Java fern (*Microsorium pteropus*), *Nitella* spp., water sprite (*Ceratopterus thalictroides* and *Ceratophyllum pteridoides*), *Cryptocoryne* spp., hornwort (*Ceratophyllum submersum*), *Anubias* spp., or other plants should be added to the breeding aquarium to provide shade and a roof for the nest, and to absorb toxic ammonia and growth-inhibiting nitrates produced by fish metabolism. Twigs, dried hardwood leaves, and peat moss leak tannic and humic acids that stain the water and lower the pH; their slow decay provides protozoans and rotifers for fry, and surface areas for nitrogen cycle bacteria. The acidity shifts the ammonia-ammonium equilibrium toward nontoxic ammonium.

Sexes should be conditioned separately with live foods, and the female should be introduced gradually to the male, either in an adjacent glass compartment or with a refugium of caves, dense vegetation, and leaf and twig litter. For her safety and that of the fry, the female should be removed after spawning. For further safety of the fry, the male should be removed when the fry can swim unassisted.

The tank should be covered to keep the adult fish from jumping out when chased or startled, to retain humidity during labyrinth development of the young fish, to exclude airborne oil-laden dust from coating

Betta anabatoides habitat at Taxan, Kalimantan, Borneo.

the surface and blocking oxygen and carbon dioxide exchange with the atmosphere, and to provide a dead-air space above the water as a temperature buffer.

Because the *splendens* group produce small fry, you will have lower mortality if they are fed infusoria (rotifers such as *Branchionus* or ciliates such as *Paramecium*) the first week or two, with live brine shrimp (*Artemia*) nauplii feeding begun on the third or fourth day they are free-swimming. As the young grow, sorting them by size into other tanks will minimize cannibalism and stunting caused by growth-inhibiting substances released by the fastest growing individuals.

Some bubblenesters use floating vegetation as support structures for their bubblenests; others construct their nest well beneath the surface under leaves or in a cave. You can add nest support structures such as sliced Styrofoam cups, whole opaque plastic jars, or 35-mm film canisters. For fish that build bubblenests far below the surface, you can provide clay flowerpots laid on their sides, or 6 inch (15 cm) segments of 0.75 inch (2 cm) diameter PVC pipes. Many bettas switch between surface and bottom nesting and use what is available. In cold months, the tank should have a low wattage heater (2.5 watts per gallon) and ther-

---

Stunting

Stunting is caused by crowding in two ways. First, the fastest growing fish in a tank emits substances that stunt its cohorts (brothers and sisters of the same spawn). The nature of these substances is unknown, but they appear to be species-specific and probably hormonal. The second is by the accumulation of nitrates, resulting from the activity of nitrogen cycle bacteria converting ammonia to nitrite and nitrite to nitrate. Breeders maximize growth by frequently or continually changing water to dilute both the nitrates and the hormonal inhibitors, and by sorting fishes by size in different tanks. With the largest fish removed, the next healthiest undergo growth spurts.

---

mometer adjusted to 80°F (27°C) and inspected daily for deviations.

If a species has not yet spawned in captivity, its relationships may tell us if it is a bubblenester or mouthbrooder. If it is a member of a species group, that might tell us about its preferred habitat. The text below presents related species by groups. Many species are not members of a group and are treated individually. To locate a species by its name, use the index.

Splendens Group

The *splendens* group ranges from Thailand southward through the western Malay peninsula and across the Strait of Melaka (= Molluca, = Malacca) to adjacent parts of Sumatra. A report from Borneo is probably a human introduction.

Betta splendens

B. splendens is native to southern, central, and eastern Thailand, Cambodia, and southern Vietnam. The other members of the *splendens* group are *B. imbellis, B. smaragdina*, and *B.* sp. Mahachai. Certain stocks have a mixed or questionable heritage, because plakat enthusiasts trade and release fish everywhere, hybridize strains that might be different species or subspecies, and fail to record the origins and release locales of their fish. The human transplantation of fighting fishes throughout Southeast Asia makes many distributional records suspect. As a result, we know more about the distribution

Habitat of Betta sp. *"Mahachai."*

of the least popular bettas than of the most popular. Hybrids confound understanding. The new pineapple betta is a tan-bodied, yellow-finned, short-fin fighter that may be a strain of *B. splendens* or a hybrid. The copper betta is certainly a hybrid. The Indo betta is a uniformly dark, almost blue-black fish, of undocumented but clearly hybrid origin.

Betta sp. Mahachai

B. sp. Mahachai is a new introduction to the United States. For many years it was known to fighting fish (plakat) breeders all over Thailand who would travel to the Mahachai-Ban Paow area near Bangkok in Samut Sakom Province of central Thailand for this fish. *Betta* sp. Mahachai occurs about 20 miles (30 km) from Bangkok near Mahachai. It builds minute bubblenests in the axils between the leaf and crown of the palm tree *Nypa fruitcans,* an upper estuary palm that is the dominant tree in a coastal swamp where pH is about 7.8. Other fishes here are *Trichopsis vittatus, Trichogaster sumatranus, Aplocheilax panchax, Channa striata, Anabas testudineus*, and a small shrimp. There are no marine-origin fish species in this habitat, and this betta does not occur in the lower, more saline estuary where those fishes do occur. Wild fish are used for fighting and for hybridizing with both *B. imbellis* and *B. splendens*, the hybrids said

Male **Betta imbellis** *"Marang."*

to have excellent fighting abilities. *B. sp.* Mahachai is easily bred in captivity with a little salt added to the water. It is dark blue-green, resembling *B. smaragdina* (but thicker) or *B. imbellis* (without red markings). Wild and market fish are similar, as are their hybrids.

Pair of **Betta imbellis** *"Marang" spawning.*

The name *Betta marchei* should not be confused with *B. sp.* Mahachai. *Betta marchei* was a name coined by Sauvage in 1878 for a fish that is probably a member of the *splendens* group, but because we cannot be certain which species it represents, that name is not in use.

Betta imbellis

B. imbellis LADIGES, 1975 is native to northeastern Sumatra, the Malay Peninsula, Penang Island, and Phuket and Ko Samui islands off Thailand. The almost black population at Ko Samui Island is endangered. A report of *Betta Imbellis* on Borneo may be a misidentification or a human transplant. The imported populations are called blue M1, Marang, Sungei Semberong, Slim River, Kuantan, Ko Samui, Nhakan Si Thamarat, and Penang.

B. imbellis occurs in swamps, rice paddies, ditches, canals, pig wallows, and flooded waterways. Tony Tejavej found some in the axils of (probably) sago palm (*Metroxylon sagu*) in upper estuarine habitat similar to that of *B. sp.* Mahachai. In its typical freshwater habitat, the water is murky or clear, up to 2 feet (0.6 m) deep, pH 5.5–7.0, 74–93°F (23–34°C), and 5–20 (perhaps higher in upper estuaries) in calcium-magnesium hardness.

Attaining about 2 inches (5 cm) total length, *B. imbellis* is blue-black. Its pelvic fins are red, the longest rays of the anal fin are red, and the caudal or tail fin has a broad, red submarginal band and a thin, black marginal band. The opercles or gill covers have two blue or green bars. Males have longer dorsal, anal, and caudal fins than females. Females develop vertical white blotches in breeding (nuptial) coloration.

B. imbellis is a short-fin fish bred for fighting, and has a reputation as a faster and more unpredictable combatant. A long-fin variety is not yet in the hobby in the United States.

B. imbellis raised separately and then placed together become fighters. Raised and kept together, they remain peaceful and will even spawn in a group tank beneath floating plants or structures. To induce breeding, isolate and condition the parents on live and frozen foods for 2 weeks. Then place them together (float the female in a jar until he has built a bubblenest) in a 10 gallon (38 L) or larger tank with 6 inches (15 cm) of 50 percent tap water and 50 percent reverse osmosis (RO) water, deionized (DI) water, or rainwater. Raise the temperature to 80°F (27°C). Put them together when the nest is built and he is attentive to the female. The male places the 50 to 500 eggs among the bubbles. The parents do not eat their young, but remove the female anyway. When the fry are free-swimming, remove the male. Start the fry on infusoria, or substitute a liquid or powder artificial diet. Begin live brine shrimp nauplii at day 3 or 4. The fry grow rapidly, but are sensitive to changes in water quality and may die as a result of a sudden water change during the first 2 months, during which time you should replace old

Copper Bettas

New types of betta on the market are the copper or copper-gold plakat and its variants, "blue face" and "indo." The copper plakat is robust and has iridocytes in the flank scales. It was derived by crossing a copper or iridocyte-rich *B. imbellis* with a fighting or plakat *B. splendens,* resulting in a copper hybrid for the fighting and decorative markets. Copper bettas are expensive, but the price will come down when suppliers begin to release females now withheld to control the market. Tony Pinto thinks the copper betta resembles the Schmidt-Focke neon betta of the 1970s–1980s, which was a hybrid of fancy *B. splendens* and wild *B. imbellis*. Tony Tejavej thinks the copper betta is a hybrid of *B. imbellis* and fancy *B. splendens*. According to this view, the "mask" of these fish is derived from the blue face of a solid turquoise *B. splendens,* but the body is from a wild plakat. The "indo" form may be a triple hybrid of *B. splendens, B. imbellis, and B.* sp. Mahachai, with a disproportionately robust body. A solution to the origins of these hybrids might be available from Wang (2002), who developed a PC-compatible computer program that estimates inbreeding in a single individual and the relatedness of two individuals using genetic markers and statistical analyses. It is free to university researchers.

Hardness

Hardness can be confusing if you use the old German aquarium literature of GH, DH, KH, and GdH. Forget those terms. All you need to know is that hardness is the concentration of (mostly) calcium and magnesium cations (Ca++, Mg++), derived from the dissolution of rocks. The rocks may be made of calcium sulfates, calcium oxides, calcium carbonates, magnesium sulfates, or magnesium carbonates. The cation concentration in nature tells you about the rocks and water quality, and it can be important because it affects a fish's ability to use its gills and the viability of eggs. Some fishes require water with a high cation concentration (hard water such as that found in limestone sinks) and others just the opposite (soft water such as rain water). I prefer to use calcium-magnesium hardness in this book as a substitute for those Germanic terms that refer to this aspect of water quality.

"Carbonate hardness" is the concentration of carbonic acid anions (COO⁻) that provide an alkaline reserve. This alkaline reserve is the capacity of anions like carbonates to neutralize acids, substances with positive charges. We often abbreviate acids with the sign for their most important components, their protons (H+). So alkalinity is the buffering capacity of the water against becoming acidic.

The term "total hardness" is the calcium and magnesium cations plus less common cations, so it is always a higher number.

Calcium-magnesium hardness usually derives from water seeping through limestone-containing rocks, but it can also come from sea water, which is why marine aquarists also measure hardness. Hard corals remove calcium and magnesium as they grow, and these substances have to be replaced by kalkwasser (calcium solution water) to keep the sea water hardness up to normal for coral and fish health.

Finally, alkaline is not the same as basic. "Basic" refers to a pH value above 7.0. Water with a high pH is basic, not alkaline.

water or add to the water level by slowly siphoning new water from above through airline tubing.

Betta smaragdina

B. smaragdina LADIGES, 1972 has a dark body with rows of metallic blue-black, blue, or green scales extending to the gill covers. Males have slightly longer fins and deeper coloration. The only red is on the pelvic fins, and they may be tipped in white. The fish attains 2.5 inches (7 cm) and looks like a smaller, slimmer, jeweled B. splendens, with prettier females. It occurs in open, grassy marshes; rice paddies; ditches; and pools that reconnect during the rainy season.

B. smaragdina occurs from Laos to the northern Thailand provinces of Nhong Khai, Udon Thani, Khon Khaen, and Ubonratchathani on the Korat Plateau.

B. smaragdina is bred for the fighting market (short fins) and the aquarium market (long fins). The most aggressive fighters are reported from Udon Thani, south of Nong Khai Province.

This fish breeds readily. A tank can have up to several females but only one male. It should be densely vegetated, and water quality should approximate a calcium-magnesium hardness of 8–10, pH 6.5–7.0, and a temperature of 75–82°F (24–28°C), with the higher temperatures for spawning. Begin with 6 inches (15 cm) of water (half RO and half aged tap water) in a 10 gallon (38 L) or larger tank so you won't have to transfer the growing fry. This bubblenester uses either underwater caves (flowerpots, PVC tubes, coconut shells) or surface vegetation (such as water sprite), and is peaceful provided the female is receptive. If she is not ready, the male may damage or kill her, so provide hiding places for her safety. Spawns are small, with only 50–150 eggs that hatch in 30 hours at 77°F (25°C). The fry are free-swimming after 3 days. The male should now be removed and the fry started on infusoria and microworms. Then, 2 days later, begin feeding newly hatched brine shrimp. Raise the water level slowly as they grow. Maturity is reached at 6 months. As they mature or "sex out," remove the males to separate jars to preserve good finnage.

Bellica Group

The two species of this group (*Betta bellica* and *B. simorum*) share large size (4–5 inch [10–15 cm]), elongated central rays in the caudal fin, and a distribution that includes the Malay Peninsula and northeastern Sumatra across the Melaka Strait.

Betta bellica

B. bellica SAUVAGE, 1884 was first reported in the nineteenth century from a swamp forest in Perak Province, 30 miles (49 km) from the Besae River in north Selangor Province on the Malay peninsula. It was rediscovered and redescribed in 1996 by Tan and Ng, who determined that the fish called *Betta fasciata* from Deli (Medan) In Sumatra was Identical, so

Betta bellica, *an unusually large bubblenester.*

Species Name

A species name consists of four parts: the genus, the specific epithet, the person who first named the fish, and the year that name was first published. The genus and specific epithet are, by convention, italicized. If the person's name is in parentheses, it means that he originally described the species in a different genus (which may no longer be valid). The Rules of Zoological Nomenclature are not complicated, but they are strict. You can order a copy from *www.iczn.org/code.htm.*

In proper usage, "sp. aff." means that this yet unnamed fish is related to a valid species whose specific epithet follows. The term "cf." means that the fish merely resembles the species indicated by the specific epithet that follows. In aquarium literature (including this book), this distinction is rarely observed, and the terms are used interchangeably.

B. fasciata is now an invalid synonym of *B. bellica,* and we know that the species ranges over most of the Malay peninsula and across the Strait of Melaka to Sumatra.

B. bellica lives in acidic blackwater streams of peat swamp forests, where it eats nymphs of damselflies and dragonflies. In various locations it has been found with *B. tussyae, B. waseri, B. hipposideros, B. livida, B. imbellis, B. persephone,* and *B.* cf. *pugnax.* At more than 4 inches (10 cm) in length, it is the largest bubblenester and is robust. It has been introduced to Thailand and other Asian locales, and there is even a release in the Dominican Republic in the Caribbean.

B. bellica is brown with iridescent green scales on the body. The color is more prominent in males, which also have longer, unpaired fins. Both the anal fin and the lanceolate caudal fin have a broad green outer band in some strains. A recently imported iridescent purple fish is called *B. bellica* (from) Muar. It isn't clear whether it was collected from the Muar River basin draining much of the south-central Malay Peninsula or specifically from the Muar River mouth at Bandar Maharani (also called Muar) on the Strait of Melaka.

Despite their large size, a 10 gallon (38 L) covered tank is sufficient for a pair, but a 20 gallon (76 L) tank provides important growing room for the fry. Provide water of low to moderate calcium-magnesium hardness (a third to a half tap water, the rest distilled or rain water), abundant surface vegetation (water sprite) to support the large bubblenest, submerse vegetation (Java moss or *Vesicularia,* coontail or *Myriophyllum*), and dried hardwood leaves, which leak tannins and acidify the water. In Asia (and in some fish rooms in the United States), breeders add dried Asian *Pandanus* and/or *Terminalia* (Indian almond) tree leaves. The male can be aggressive, so add hiding places for the female (flowerpots, PVC tubes, driftwood, and Java moss).

Feed with live and frozen foods, and siphon feces and uneaten food from the bottom. The water quality parameters can vary: pH 4.4–7.5, calcium-magnesium hardness near 15, temperature 81–84°F (27–29°C), and conductivity 33 mS. Although it occurs in nature in acidic water, *B. bellica* does better in captivity at neutral pH. The bubblenest is made of large bubbles, and the fry at hatching are enormous (0.3 inch [1 cm]) and able to consume live *Artemia* nauplii as soon as they are free-swimming, so infusoria (*Paramecium* and similar small organisms) are not needed. The larger the breeding tank, the more fry you might raise. If spawned in a smaller (10 gallon [38 L]) tank, remove some fry every 2 weeks and divide them among more tanks.

Betta simorum

B. simorum TAN AND NG, 1996 was described from a peat swamp forest draining into the Batang Hari and Indragiri Rivers in Jambi and adjacent Riau Provinces near the east coast of central Sumatra. These shallow blackwater sites had thick layers of leaf litter on the bottom and overhanging riparian (streamside) trees that shaded the streams from the equatorial sun. Other fishes in these cool, slow to stagnant waters were *B. coccina, B. cf. fusca, B. renata, Parosphromenus sumatranus, Belontia hasselti, Trichogaster leeri,* and *Sphaerichthys osphromenoides.*

Like *B. bellica, B. simorum* is a large bubblenester with iridescent

Conductivity

Conductivity is a measure of the dissolved charged ions in water. These charged ions or electrolytes affect the strength and distance of an alternating electrical current passed from one metal pole to another. Conductivity is important when collecting fishes with an electric shocking device. If conductivity is low (as in rain water), more current is needed to send a charge from the positive pole to the negative pole, in order to shock nearby fish into unconsciousness. If the conductivity is high, as in hard water from limestone areas, less current is applied in order not to kill everything between the anode and cathode. If conductivity is extremely high, as in sea water, electric shockers can't be used. We measure conductivity in units called micro Siemens per centimeter (mS/cm) or thousands of a Siemen per centimeter. It's an arcane measure of electrolytes that's related to hardness, but it has practical value for scientists who often make collections with electric shockers.

green scales. The species are similar. However, when a large series of both species were compared, they differed consistently in meristics (scale and fin ray counts). In addition, in *B. simorum* the elongate pelvic fins extend back to the middle of the anal fin (as opposed to barely reaching that fin), the head is slightly smaller, the head profile is straight (as opposed to slightly rounded in *B. bellica*), and the protruding central caudal fin rays are longer. Although usually green or brown, a blue form that appeared briefly in the hobby apparently has been lost.

The water quality in the native habitat was pH 4.5, calcium-magnesium hardness 1, alkalinity 1, temperature 81°F (27°C), and conductivity was low. In aquaria, keep the pH at 6.0–7.0 and the temperature at 72–79°F (22–26°C). Feed live and frozen foods, use a large covered tank to prevent the fish from jumping out, add abundant vegetation for hiding places, and acidify and stain the water with dried hardwood leaves. The breeding setup is the same as described for *B. bellica*, but males are not as aggressive and females are not usually damaged.

Coccina Group

Betta coccina is typical of a group of small, slender, elongate bettas, usually deep red on the body and fins (blue-black in *B. persephone*). They may have a blue-green blotch on the middle of the flank in one sex (*B. coccina*), both sexes (*B. livida, B. brownorum*), or not at all (*B. rutilans, B. persephone, B. miniopinna, B. tussyae, B. burdigala*). Their gill covers may have red or yellow bars. They have 9 abdominal vertebrae versus 10 or 11 in all other species of *Betta*.

The *coccina* species live in stenotopic (rigidly unvarying) semiaquatic habitats consisting of small, shallow pools within almost stagnant streams that seep through the ancient peat forest floor. The water is strongly acidic and almost black. Similar habitat is used also by the *waseri* group. The *coccina* group ranges from the southern Malay Peninsula to Sumatra, and to northern Borneo north of the Kapuas River. In short, they exist wherever ancient peat forests still persist in South Asia.

B. coccina survive because the acidic water is so extreme that it is unfavorable for competitors and predators, so predation is limited, and localized drought and lowering of the water table are the greater threats. The species may also survive here (and this is pure speculation) because their predominant red and iridescent green colors are warnings (poster colors) signaling predators that they have a noxious taste from eating ants. That is the explanation of poster colors in South American dart frogs that live in similarly restrictive habitats in Central America and eat ants for nutrition. David Armitage, who has collected them in the wild, has suggested that red color and the reflective green spot may be visual signals in dim light and dark water.

These peat forest pools sit atop 2 inch (5 cm) thick layers of packed leaf litter that are penetrated by *Cryptocoryne* and *Nymphaea* and grow to heights reflecting fluctuating water levels. The tannic and humic acids leached from the peat and leaf litter depress the pH to 5.5–3.5.

How to Make Low pH Blackwater

You can adjust RO water that you make or DI or distilled water that you purchase to a lower pH and darken it by adding commercial blackwater tonic. Two to four drops of Seaquarium's Humaquat in 5 gallons (19 L) will drop the pH from neutral to 5.0. When using chemicals for pH adjustment, always check the results with a pH test kit. I adjust my RO water to low pH and tint it with the tannic and humic acids from peat moss and dried oak leaves and twigs. I fill a 30 gallon (114 L) plastic trash barrel with RO water and empty a small sack (5 pound [2 kg]) of peat moss and an armful of dry hardwood leaves into the water. I sink the leaves with small branches and aerate the water constantly to keep the mix from becoming stagnant, polluted, and malodorous. The aeration ensures that leaf decomposition is aerobic, with the side benefit that ciliates and rotifers (infusoria) grow on the leaf and twig surfaces. Within 2 weeks, the water is dark and acidic, but clean, clear, and free from bad odors. I use this water to make partial water changes and to add to newly set-up RO tanks with a gallon or so of blackwater. I add more RO water to make up for what I remove. I maintain 24 10 gallon (38 L) tanks and another dozen smaller tanks for these small bettas and for licorice gouramies, and one barrel provides all my blackwater needs. (I also use it to make dark, acidic water for spawning tetras.) I connected my RO unit's discharge port to a barrel for pure RO water, but can transfer the discharge line into the blackwater barrel. I extend the RO unit tubes with flexible quarter-inch ice-maker tubing from an appliance or hardware store. You can also use this tubing to discharge the unit's waste effluent of concentrated (hard) water to another barrel for rainbow fish or for African lake cichlid water, or you can pipe it to a sink for disposal.

Roads through these forests may have drainage ditches alongside in which these fish also occur. Sometimes the roads parallel deeper, slowly flowing streams up to 2 feet (0.6 m) deep. Ephemeral (seasonal) overflow ponds and wet depressions are common on the forest floor. Most of the ephemeral ponds fill from flooding streams that replenish them with perennial fishes such as anabantoids (especially *Belontia, Anabas, Trichogaster, Trichopsis, Parosphromenus,* and *Helostoma), Rasbora*, and siluroids (catfishes) capable of air breathing. Rainfall and river flooding may provide continuous replenishment of the pools with clean water.

B. coccina eat terrestrial ants and mites. Unlike other bubblenesters,

Betta coccina *(common form).*

they do not abandon or eat their off-spring. In aquaria they may form family groups that jointly defend a territory. Allan and Barbara Brown seldom found more than one or two pairs in a pool. Because the fish are territorial, he doubts they form family groups in the wild. Occasional and intermittent mouthbrooding, in response to disturbances, has been reported in *B. rutilans* and some other species of this group. Mouth-brooding may be more common in these fishes than we know.

It was the *coccina* group that prompted the revolutionary study by Witte and Schmidt upon which all *Betta* taxonomy (scientific classifica-tion) is based. The species in this group generally do not have overlap-ping distributions. People who have bred the species in captivity have been unable to produce hybrids.

Betta coccina

B. coccina VIERKE, 1979 was dis-covered in a commercial importation, and its original location is unknown. It is reddish brown to wine red, and the male has a square, iridescent green blotch on the middle of the flank. Donoso (1989) examined all reports of collections and concluded that *B. coccina* occurs in a small part of the lowlands on the west side of the Malay Peninsula near Muar and from Jambi on adjacent Sumatra. The related *B. tussyae* occurs on the east side of the Malay Peninsula, the two species separated by a moun-tain range. Linke collected it in clear untinted water, and in black, soft, acidic (pH 4.0–5.0) water.

Early importations often died of stress-induced velvet disease (*Pisci-noodinium*). Donoso (1989) had a velvet infestation that he treated by raising the temperature to 93°F (34°C), after which the temperature was reduced to 77–84°F (25–29°C), and the fish recovered.

B. coccina spawns under surface leaves, inside floating PVC tubes or film canisters, and in other tight hid-ing places. Tony Pinto found the males aggressive during spawning (he uses 5 gallon [19 L] tanks), but the parents did not eat eggs or fry that grew up in the spawning tanks. *B. coccina* can breed to at least 3 years of age, and fish younger than a year old produce smaller spawns. Pinto used DI water adjusted to pH 5.2 and blackened with wood extract. Donoso's breeders took frozen brine shrimp, bloodworms, small insects, and mysids, but ignored tubifex worms and daphnia. The females developed a bright green horizontal line in breeding condition, and the male's square green blotch was enhanced with white edging. These fish produced small spawns (30–60 eggs yielding perhaps 10 fry) in small (less than 2 inches [5 cm] wide, one or two bubbles deep) bubblenests, and the fry were delicate, but the parents spawned frequently. The fry take *Artemia* nauplii at once, but several people start them on infusoria, green water, Liquifry, or powdered food.

Several stocks are in the hobby. The fish labeled *B. burdigala* from Banka, Indonesia, in Frank Schäfer's Aqualog is believed to be *B. coccina* from Pangkalanbun. Other stocks originated in Jambi in Sumatra and Muar in Johore in the south of the Malay Peninsula, and there is a "lancet fin" from a commercial importation of unknown origin. Keep these stocks unmixed, in case they are found to represent distinct species.

Betta livida

B. livida NG AND KOTTELAT, 1992 is red with an iridescent green midlateral blotch in both sexes, deep maroon fins with iridescent green streaks, green tips on the pelvic fins (not white as in *B. brownorum*), two vertical gold bars on the gill cover, and 10 or 11 dorsal fin rays. It occurs in blackwater streams and pools in peat forests in north Selangor Province on the central west coast of the Malay Peninsula. It was found along the road from Sanjung Malim and Tanjong Malim to the Besar River, and along the Rawang-Kuala Lumpur road in a pool surrounded by

Betta coccina, *wild form from Sumatra (Indonesia).*

Pandanus trees. *B. livida* ranges from the Kuala Selangor area northward, whereas *B. persephone* occurs to the south in the Johore region and on the opposite side of the peninsula from *B. tussyae* of the Pahang area on the east coast.

It lives in shallow (3 feet [1 m]) blackwater streams and pools among plant debris, or at the edges of deeper streams. The water was reported as pH 3.5–3.7 and tea colored, and barely flowing or not. Other fish in more open waters included *Anabas testudineus, Belontia hasselti, Sphaerichthys osphromenoides, Trichogaster leeri, T. pectoralis, T. trichopterus, Trichopsis vittata*, an unnamed member of the *B. waseri* group, *Helostoma temmincki*, and *Luciocephalus pulcher*. The water at the *Pandanus* tree location was light brown to clear, pH 4.5–5.5, and contained *Parosphromenus harveyi* and other fishes.

Two stocks in the hobby are called "Tanjong Malim Selangor" and "Selangor Forest." Both may be

Betta brownorum, *wild, with central green mark.*

the same fish from the same location under different codes. In any case, the fish is endemic to the Selangor River drainage and possibly the Buloh River drainage immediately to the south in Selangor Province.

Betta brownorum

B. brownorum WITTE AND SCHMIDT, 1992, the most beautiful of the *coccina* group, occurs in the floodplain

Betta brownorum, *wild, without a central green mark.*

of the Sarawak River near Matang, west of Kuching, in Sarawak on the north end of Borneo.

In both sexes the body is deep wine red with a green midlateral blotch (slightly less pronounced in females), the dorsal fin has 10–11 rays, the leading pelvic fin rays are white, and the iris is iridescent blue.

Good health requires strongly acidic water, also needed for maintaining the stickiness of the bubblenest. At spawning the nest may be incomplete, but enlarged afterward. Eggs hatch in 36 hours, and the fry are free-swimming and start feeding at 130 hours. In response to disturbances, the male may take the eggs or larvae into his mouth and move them to another location where he builds another nest. Sometimes he holds them for protracted periods, leading some to suggest that at least one stock may be mouthbrooders. The female defends the territory and the male guards the nest. Larger fry do not feed on younger siblings, and a family of mixed ages and sizes may defend a territory. Brian Ahmer removed the eggs at spawning, but they failed to hatch. Subsequently, he removed the parents after the eggs hatched and about 30 fry survived.

Maturity is reached in 6 months, maximum size (2 inches [5 cm]) is reached in a year, and the life span is at least 5 years. The bubblenesting stocks in the hobby are "Matang" and "Sibu," and there is also an unnamed mouthbrooding form.

Betta rutilans

B. rutilans WITTE AND KOTTELAT in Kottelat, 1991 is small (1.5 inches [3 cm]), slender, and deep red (both sexes) with no distinctive green blotch on the flank. Juveniles are striped. It differs from *B. tussyae* in one rather than two dorsal fin spines, two rather than three anal fin spines, and differs from all other *Betta* species in having fused hypural (tail fin) plates six and seven.

The species is native to streams of the Pinyuh and Kepayang Rivers, northeast of Pontianak and south-east of Anjungan in West Kaliman-tan, Borneo. Linke found it in a marshy, low conductivity (39 mS), acidic (pH 4.5) stream with clear, dark brown water, where it feeds on bloodworms (chironomid fly larvae), mites, and ostracods.

B. rutilans may spawn repeatedly in an acidic tank with dense vegeta-tion, leaves, twigs, and a diet of live food. It spawns in PVC tubes on the top or bottom, under floating styro-foam cups, or among surface vegeta-tion, especially in tank corners. I've had some success moving late-stage eggs, but best results are obtained by waiting for the eggs to hatch in the spawning tank and removing the pair when the fry are free-swimming (and seem to disappear in the vegetation). Production is about 30 eggs per spawn. At hatching, the prolarvae are incapable of swimming. If the male is disturbed, he takes fry or eggs into his mouth for safekeeping or place-ment elsewhere. In my experience, it is a bubblenester, but it may do both.

Betta rutilans, *juvenile, tank-bred.*

At other times, it may stop spawning entirely.

In the small to moderately sized bubblenest, the fry repeatedly fall and are retrieved and returned by the male. Eventually, the fry leave the tube or nest and hang vertically from an adjacent leaf by their heads, suggesting cement head glands, as described by Jones (1940) and sup-ported by Britz et al. (2001), who called these glands attachment organs. Cement glands, or attach-ment organs, are more important than bubblenest mucus in providing support for the *coccina* group.

Don't merely add water to the grow-out tank to make up for evap-oration (which increases hardness), but instead remove large amounts of water to be replaced with new makeup water. This species toler-ates hard water, but doesn't grow quickly, develop deep colors, or spawn under those conditions. When raised together in a grow-out tank, the fry grow at various rates to different maximum sizes. For best survival and most even growth, house the juveniles at one fish per 1 gallon (4 L) jar, with abundant vegetation and snails to keep the aquarium clean of leftover food.

Betta sp. aff. *rutilans* "Green" resembles *B. rutilans* except that its body is adorned with iridescent green scales. There is no information about its hypural plates or its origin, but Ralph Tran believes that it was collected in the same waters with the standard *B. rutilans*, that it may be a mouthbrooder, and that it probably represents an unnamed species.

Betta persephone

B. persephone SCHALLER, 1986 attains a length of only 1.5 inches (3 cm). The body is slender, brown, slate gray, greenish black, or bluish black. The unpaired fins are blue (sometimes with a flush of red in the fin membranes), and the pelvic fins may be uniformly dark or red with white tips. The iris of the eye is iridescent blue. In nuptial coloration,

Betta persephone, *male.*

the male is more brightly colored, but otherwise the sexes are similar.

B. persephone occurs in the southwest of the Malay Peninsula. The strain "Muar" denotes the Segamat-Muar area in Johor, not far from where the types were discovered along Asian Highway Number 2, about 1.5 miles (2.5 km) north of Ayer Hitam (which means "black water").

B. persephone was placed on the IUCN Red List of threatened species at the urging of Dr. Maurice Kottelat, largely based on threats to its ancient peat forest habitat from logging. It occurs among leaves, roots, and leaf litter in soft, black, acidic water of floodplains, and may survive low-water periods by finding water beneath damp leaves. It will not survive in or on damp mud.

Maintain one pair or trio in a densely planted tank with RO water, peat moss, twigs, and dried hardwood leaves to generate tannins and a final pH of 5.0–5.5 or less. The peat moss and leaves will leach and turn the water tea colored to almost black. The acidity will protect the fish from waste ammonia that converts to harmless ammonium. Feed live foods only. The male may use a floating tube for refuge and build its nest in the tube or outside and adjacent, or he may select a sunken tube. Spawns number about 40 eggs, and the fry initially feed on infusoria or a dried equivalent (APR, or artificial plankton rotifer) before they take live brine shrimp nauplii. The surfaces of the dead leaves and live vegetation generate gliding protozoa, and no other infusoria should be necessary. Fry can be left with the parents and with previous spawns in a family tank, because cannibalism seems not to occur (Pinto, 2000). I've also had best production leaving the young with the parents. Growth is slow, and maturity is attained in 9 months, at which time the males may become territorial. The fish tolerates hard water, but does not grow well or spawn in these conditions, even with abundant space.

Pair of Betta persephone, *male above.*

Betta miniopinna

B. miniopinna TAN AND TAN, 1994 was discovered at Tanjungpinang on Bintan Island in the Riau Island group east of Singapore. It was collected in shaded, acidic waters in a swamp forest with leaf litter and soft mud substratum.

Recently, the name was reported to be a synonym of *B. persephone.* Although there are similarities in coloration between some *B. persephone* and *B. miniopinna* males, other *B. miniopinna* males resemble *B. coccina* in ruddy coloration and striping, conditions that do not occur in *B. persephone.* Based on photographs and the geographic location of this island population, I consider *B. miniopinna* a valid species. *B. miniopinna* is on the IUCN Red List as critically endangered.

Betta tussyae

B. tussyae SCHALLER, 1985 lacks the green central flank spot common to many members of the *coccina*

group. It was collected 48 miles (77 km) south of Kuantan along a road 0.5 mile (1 km) inland and 11 miles (18 km) south of Pekan in Pahang state on the east side of the Malay Peninsula. The water in these small, barely flowing or stagnant streams was darkly stained with tannins, the pH 5.5, the calcium-magnesium hardness 1–2 (extremely soft), and the temperature 77°F (25°C). There were dense aquatic vegetation and dead leaves beneath overhanging terrestrial streamside vegetation.

Betta miniopinna *from Bintan Island.*

Betta tussyae.

Linke also found it in stagnant shore-line coves of larger forest streams with strong midchannel flow, again among dead leaves, forest litter, and dense vegetation, where the pH was often less than 4.0. The fish has also been found near Kuantan on the Kuantan-Segamat Road, in a stream less than 6 feet (2 m) deep, in water at pH 5.5, 15 mS (extremely low conductivity), and tea colored from tannins (Krummenacher 1985, cited in Linke 1991). Other localities for *B. tussyae* were out in the open in full sunlight at the forest's edge, but the water flowing out of the forest was exceptionally acidic at pH 3.62. Many other anabantoid fishes occurred in these same streams, including *Sphaerichthys osphromenoides, Parosphromenus nagyi, Trichopsis vittatus, Channa, Betta imbellis,* and *Betta pugnax.* Populations of *B. tussyae* have been collected from locales known as MK 314, km 310 Mersing-Johor-Baru, M14+M16 (Donoso, 1989), Rompin (IBC), and Chukai—the latter collected by Pinto and Yong in 2000 and brought into the hobby.

Betta burdigala

B. burdigala KOTTELAT AND NG, 1994 was discovered by the aquarist Neugenbauer in a secondary growth, flooded peat swamp forest less than 2 miles (3 km) north of Bikang on the road from Koba to Toboali on Bangka Island, 15 miles (24 km) off the east coast of Sumatra. The fish were collected during high water among tree and plant roots. His water quality measurements were pH 3.78, conductivity 20 mS, and temperature 75°F (24°C).

Like other members of the *coccina* group, *B. burdigala* is wine red (*burdigala* is Latin for "Bordeaux"), with three dark red stripes on the head. Seldom is a fish so distinctive to aquarists and ichthyologists alike. It is the only member of the *coccina* group with iridescent green patches on the first third of the dorsal and anal fins, and its dorsal fin has a thin white margin. It has 8 or 9 abdominal vertebrae as compared to 10 or

Male Betta burdigala.

11 in all other *Betta* species, and a total dorsal fin ray count of 14 or 15 elements as compared with 10 or 11 in other members of the *coccina* group and 7 to 11 in all other *Betta* species. It attains a length of 2.5 inches (6.5 cm).

Males have slightly longer and more pointed dorsal and anal fins and slightly deeper coloration. A pair can be housed in a 5 gallon (19 L) tank with soft, acidic water no more than 5 inches (12.5 cm) deep, pH 4.0–5.5, low calcium-magnesium hardness (about 1 or 2), conductivity less than 100 mS, temperature of 71–75°F (22–24°C), abundant vegetation such as Java moss and water sprite, dead leaves, twigs, live foods, and little or no aeration. Poor water quality may lead to fin rot, but weekly 30-percent water changes will prevent fin damage and may induce breeding.

The male builds a substantial bubblenest before or during spawning. The pair will spawn in a floating black 35-mm film canister, a floated PVC tube (attached to styrofoam), or beneath floating plants. Spawning may be repeated at 2-week intervals. After spawning, the female guards the territory and the male tends the eggs. If disturbed, the male may take the eggs in his mouth to move elsewhere or hold them up to 4 days, time enough for hatching. The eggs and young usually do best left with the parents, but some males eat the eggs. You can remove the eggs from the nest and transfer them for incubation in shallow dishes with acriflavine added to tank water. The fry are free-swimming after 5 days. The parents can also be kept in a larger tank (and will breed) occupied by small rasboras, such as *Microrasbora maculata, Rasbora axelrodi,* and *Boraras bridgetti. B. burdigala* is on the IUCN Red List of threatened species.

Related Species or Possible Variants

Betta cf. *burdigala* "Kubu" attains 2 inches (5 cm) but is mature at much less, and has slightly different fin and ray counts. The body has blue-green iridescent scales, and the fins are red. The head may be bright red. Females are duller, smaller, and have shorter unpaired fins that are dark red with white spots. The iris is iridescent blue in both sexes. This fish was found in shallow water with abundant vegetation and fallen

Betta sp. *"Sukadana"* of the coccina group.

Forest floor habitat of Betta *sp. "Pankalanbun."*

leaves according to Stefan van der Voort (2003). The fish were kept at pH 5.0, calcium-magnesium hardness 1–2, and 77–81°F (25–27°C). The tank also had dried oak leaves and peat moss. Hiding places were provided, and black film canisters were provided for spawning sites. The plants were Java fern, Java moss, and two kinds of *Anubias*. The fish ate mosquito larvae and brine shrimp, but refused daphnia.

The male prepared a bubblenest inside a floating 35-mm film canister. The pair spawned after several days.

The Origins of Mouthbrooding?

If the observations of large fry and combined mouthbrooding and bubblenesting in *Betta rutilans* and other members of the *coccina* group are confirmed, they suggest how mouthbrooding could have evolved. The large fry indicate an adaptation to a harsh environment where size provides the young a selective advantage over smaller fry of the other anabantoids in this habitat. The advantage could be the ability to prey on those smaller fry (perhaps an abundant food source), ability to prey on larger protozoans or rotifers, or growth beyond the size selected by a local predator (another fish or even an insect). Such an early adaptation by an ancestral *Betta* would also adapt it for survival in flood zones where nests might wash away in heavy rains, and then into slow-moving streams and finally into larger, faster-flowing bodies of water.

This fish is polygamous. A male may spawn with two females at the same time using the same nest. It is also a serial spawner, with 1–2 dozen eggs (and fry) produced at a single spawning, and then another spawn within a few days.

Betta sp. "Pangkalanbun" and *Betta* sp. "Sukadana" may also be members of this group, according to Pinto and van der Voort.

Chapter Four
Mouthbrooding Bettas

The aquarist H. J. Richter proposed that mouthbrooding bettas be placed in a new, separate genus, *Pseudobetta,* with *Betta* reserved for bubblenesters. The suggestion had no merit because the first fish named *Betta* was itself a mouthbrooder, so *Betta* would have priority for mouthbrooders, and we'd need a new name for the bubblenesters (Roberts, 1989). Britz (2001) considered whether mouthbrooders were a distinct group based on the knoblike projections of their eggs as opposed to wrinkles on the egg surfaces in bubblenesters. In subsequent work, he rejected that interpretation and now believes mouthbrooding arose more than once and the egg surface differences may be adaptations to the mouth and throat environment rather than an ancestral condition. If subgenera are to be established for the genus *Betta,* they will need to be based on better evidence of relationships.

Mouthbrooder Basics

Most mouthbrooders are assigned to species groups based on morpho-logical traits, ecological characteristics (habitat similarities), and behavioral similarities, although there is no general agreement on which species are clearly in one group as opposed to another. Reflecting this disagreement, the allocations I have used in this book sometimes differ from those in Witte and in Frank Schäfer's *Aqualog* book.

Mouthbrooding *Betta* species may be as small as *B. picta* or up to 5 inches (12.5 cm) long. Many are dull gray or brown with or without iridescent green or blue scales on the body and gill covers. A few have unique patterns and beautiful coloration, but they can be more difficult to keep than the bubblenesters.

Many mouthbrooders live in flowing streams in hilly and sometimes limestone-rich regions, whereas others occur in forested lowland swamps. In upland locales, the water is often neutral (pH 6.5–7.2), with a moderate calcium-magnesium hardness and conductivity from percolation through limestone in the underlying soils and bedrock. These streams vary from bare trickles to rivers 20 feet (6 m) across. Here the mouthbrooders occupy

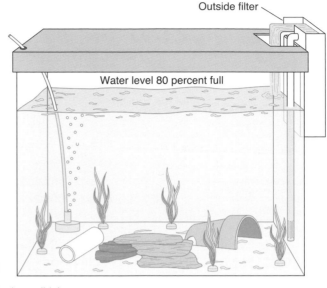

- Fish Size ⟶ Tank Size
1-3"	5-10 gal.
3-5"	20 gal.
>5"	30 gal.

- Tank Cover   Yes

- Lighting   Yes

- Surface Structures
  Not applicable

- Bottom Structures
  3-6" × 1.5" PVC tube
  Broken clay flower pot
    (widen drain hole)
  Rock cave

- Filtration
  Sponge filter (fast)
  Outside filter (floss and carbon)

- Temperature   68°-74° heater(submersible)
  pH   6.5-7.5 (no adjustment)
  Vegetation   Surface and bottom
  Gravel   Not needed

Outside filter

Water level 80 percent full

How to set up a breeding tank for mouthbrooders.

densely vegetated, slowly flowing riverbank undercuts and indentations, backwaters away from the main current, or pools and ditches off the main channel. The bottom may have more sand than mud, and usually abundant rooted and midwater vegetation instead of packed dead leaves. The streams are often shaded by overhanging riparian trees and tall grasses that drop an endless array of insects to the water below. Within these habitats, there may be ecological separation into niches. David Armitage has seen juveniles of one species sharing shaded forest floor pools with adults of a second species.

Mouthbrooding is an adaptation to flowing water. It enables fish to breed in the open where nests are indefensible, where currents would preclude bubbles, and in response to different water levels. It converts the male's buccal cavity (throat) into a mobile nest, allows the fry to develop in safety until large enough to withstand currents and feed on their own, and enables the parents to travel from spawning area to nursery area for fry release. Mouthbrooding may promote socialization by eliminating territorial defense, although some mouthbrooders, such as members of the *waseri* group, are notably territorial. Socialization may produce synchronized spawning, as discussed under *Betta picta*. Synchronized spawning is common among mouthbrooders but not bubblenesters, and may be induced by sex hormones being released in the water by some members of the group and causing behavioral responses in the others. (Unrelated *Corydoras* catfishes sharing a single multitank filtration system typically spawn at the same time, the pheromones of one spawning group inducing spawning in the others.)

Most mouthbrooders are peaceful and are not used (or trained) for fighting. Many can be kept in group tanks without danger to other individuals or other kinds of fishes. Most do well in large (20 gallon [76 L] or more), covered tanks with moderately hard water at neutral pH. They feed more heavily on live and frozen foods than bubblenesters, and can be safely fed flake and granular foods because leftovers are not likely to decay anaerobically and lower the pH in aerated hard water.

Provide many rooted plants (*Cryptocoryne* is my favorite genus), and an open area for breeding in the front and center of the tank. Include overturned flowerpots, large-diameter PVC pipe segments (3 inches [7.5 cm]), driftwood, and rocks for caves. Use sponge filters or outside power filters with activated carbon to adsorb colors and chemicals. Supplement their frozen adult brine shrimp and bloodworms with shavings of frozen edible shrimp and beef heart. The staple diet should include live black

worms or tubifex worms, white or grindal worms, and chopped earthworms. Frequent massive water changes maintain water quality and often induce spawning.

A few species are not sociable, and no more than one male should be in the tank. In general, a 20 gallon (76 L) tank is suitable for a pair, but a group with two or more males should have at least a 50 gallon (189 L) tank. All mouthbrooders are strong jumpers, and should have covered tanks.

More peaceful mouthbrooders, such as *B. picta,* are social, can be kept in large communities, and may respond to a massive (25 percent) water change with next-day, simultaneous spawning of the entire group. There is no nest, but there is a distinctive spawning area, usually in a clearing near the bottom. The female initiates spawning by poking the male. Eventually the pair embraces, with the female wrapped at a right angle within the arched body of the male, their genital orifices in apposition. They both tremble and freeze at orgasm. The curved anal fin of the now stuporous male becomes a cup, gathering the heavier-than-water eggs. As the white eggs spill over his anal fin, the female gathers them in her mouth. The male recovers more slowly. When he approaches again, she spits the eggs toward him and he catches them in his mouth for incubation. When breeding has been completed minutes or hours later, the female loses interest and the male has an enlarged throat. He then loses his nuptial colors and changes his pattern to resemble a female or juvenile, while he seeks a densely planted refuge.

In a large, well-planted tank with one pair of fish, you can allow both parents to remain after spawning and the male to brood and eventually release the fry. You will obtain better production, however, by moving him to a nursery tank where he can have privacy and then safely release the fry when fully developed. Do not move a brooding male the first few days after spawning, because the eggs are delicate and he is high-strung and might eat or abandon them. After 3–4 days, he should be netted or captured in a glass jar for removal to his own vegetated, covered, 10 gallon (38 L) tank (with aeration), and not fed. During incubation, he will "chew" and "gulp" as he rotates the eggs or fry around his throat. Between 1 and 2 weeks later, he releases the fry a few at a time or all at once. On that day, his throat shrinks to normal size, and you will see the fry on the bottom or in the vegetation. Afterward, he can be placed back into his original tank and promptly fed. The fry take newly hatched live brine shrimp or microworms as a first food, so infusoria is not necessary. Spawns range from 20–100, depending on the size and experience of the adults.

An alternative method, useful with smaller mouthbrooders, is to place the incubating male in a standard livebearer or guppy-breeding trap. The released fry fall through the grate or slot at the bottom into the box's trap or directly into a grow-out tank.

Yohan Fernando noted that some males won't hold the eggs to term, perhaps because of infertile eggs that are slow to fungus or inexperienced, or because of fright, or aggression. Whatever the reason, stripping the eggs in a manner similar to stripping mouthbrooding cichlids may be the only option. To strip a male, restrain him firmly in a net and, with your fingernail or a toothpick, pull down on the lower jaw while holding the fish under water in dim light. If you are lucky, the male will spit out the eggs as soon as he is caught in the net, but fingernail finesse may be required.

The next challenge is handling the eggs. According to Fernando, "Some breeders use egg-tumblers. I make a hatchery from a 0.5 gallon (2 L) container. First I fill the container with water from the breeding tank and insert an air stone. The airflow is adjusted with a gang valve to ensure even and constant air flow throughout the container. I place a 4 inch (10 cm) fine, smooth-mesh fish net on the container submerged about 1 inch (2.5 cm) in the water and protect the eggs from light by working in a dim room. I add an antimicrobial agent such as Maroxy or acriflavine to the container, and then pour the eggs into the net. Usually on the third day the eggs discolor. On the fourth or fifth day there is visible development of the embryos. Any that develop fungus should be immediately removed. Ten to 11 days postspawning, the fry are free-swimming and should be removed from the hatchery and put in a 2.5

Ecological Niches

Despite the usual differences between mouthbrooder and bubblenester habitats, many species occur together in the same waters. If there is only one species in a habitat, it is free to exploit all foods and space. More often, however, a *Betta* species is only one of several kinds of fishes, and sometimes of several species of *Betta* in that water body. The more species in a place (especially closely related species), the more they segregate to avoid interfering with each other for food or shoreline, deep water, leaf litter, vegetation, or any combination. When more than one *Betta* species occurs in a stream, you can bet that some species of certain sizes will be found only in leaf litter, others only in dense vegetation, and so on. In addition, one form may feed on dragonfly or damselfly larvae, another on bloodworm (chironomid fly) larvae, and others on worms or amphipods on the bottom, or on ants and mites falling from overhanging trees. This specialization to share resources and exploit the habitat is the species' ecological niche or place in the scheme of things. It is also what enables you to keep more than one species in a tank. When you cannot, it may be because they compete for the same niche.

gallon (9.5 L) aquarium. Free-swimming fry readily eat microworms and newly hatched brine shrimp. Within 3 months, the fry reach 1 inch (2.5 cm) and begin to display features of their parents." Fernando also suggests not putting all the eggs from one stripping into the same basket, but spreading the risk among several containers.

Many mouthbrooders are not yet organized into species groups, but that will change as we learn more about their relationships. Suggestions that mouthbrooding bettas should be in a separate subgenus have no scientific support. The DNA work done on relationships indicates that mouthbrooding arose more than once from bubblenesting, in itself an argument that mouthbrooders are not a single evolutionary group. In fact, bubblenesters also seem to have evolved as several groups (*coccina* group, *splendens* group, etc.), and there is neither evidence nor suggestion that bubblenesters should be constituted into a single subgenus.

Betta dimidiata:
A Betta Without
a Species Group!

B. *dimidiata* ROBERTS, 1989 lives in oxbow lakes and forested or wide-open tributaries of the Kapuas

Betta dimidiata *spawning.*

River of West Kalimantan. It was collected in the Siriang River near Sanggau-Hulu, 22 miles (35 km) west of Putussibau, downstream at Sintag, and from the Gentu, Tekam, and Ketchil Rivers.

B. dimidiata occurs sympatrically (together) with *Betta enisae* in lightly tinted brown waters at pH 5.2–6.5, calcium-magnesium hardness of 1–2, alkalinity of 1, and 20 mS conductivity.

For a mouthbrooder, this is a small fish at less than 3 inches (7.5 cm) in body length. Both sexes have a rust-brown body with a line of black blotches forming a horizontal stripe, and the anal fin has a broad iridescent metallic green submarginal band. The mature male has blue highlights in his elongated unpaired fins, and extended central rays in the spade-shaped caudal fin. Males are aggressive and might damage females in smaller tanks without dense vegeta-

tion as refuges. During breeding, the male darkens to deep reddish brown, whereas the female's black stripe intensifies. Pinto (1999) kept this mouthbrooder in RO water filtered through peat and reported that warm temperatures of 78°F (25.5°C) were necessary to maintain health and induce breeding. The male releases up to 30 minute fry after 12–14 days of incubation. They must be started on infusoria for the first week and, even after weaned to live baby brine shrimp, growth is slow. The small fry and their small number is not unexpected in a small mouthbrooder. Its extensive distribution in the massive Kapuas River and its tributaries renders it safe from exploitation, development, or natural disasters. To date, B. dimidiata has not been relegated to a species group.

Picta **Group**

The *picta* species group (B. picta, B. taeniata, B. falx, B. simplex, B. edithae, B. prima) are characterized by prominent dark margins in the anal and caudal fins, an iridescent gill cover, small size, 21–26 anal fin rays, 8–10 dorsal fin rays, 27–29 vertebrae, 27–30 lateral scales, and 5–6 subdorsal scales. That sounds technical, but when you compare their pictures, they all appear to be one closely related group.

Betta picta

B. picta CUVIER AND VALENCIENNES, 1846 was described more than a century and a half ago, but not clearly, and the type (original) specimens no longer exist. That led to some confusion. In was reported in 1846 from Buitenzorg, Java, and later, from Pajakumnbu and near Medan Deli, Sumatra. It was again cited by Bleeker in 1879 and Weber & De Beaufort in 1912 and by Kottelat and coworkers in 1993. Witte & Schmidt's (1992) *B. edithae* from the Jambi area was also probably this species. The confusion in the 1992 and 1993 reports, and the lack of types, induced Tan and Kottelat to redescribe the fish in 1998.

B. picta is an upland fish of cool mountain streams, where the water quality was described as pH 6.5–7.5, calcium-magnesium hardness of 22, and temperature of 72–75°F (22–24°C).

The colors of the (maximum size) 2.5 inch (6.5 cm) fish vary from gray with a dark back and two or three dark horizontal stripes, the middle one ending in a basicaudal spot, to almost purple with bands or blotches. The anal fin has rows of purple spots or, more commonly, a purple band from the base to at least the middle of the fin, where the fin then displays a broad blue submarginal band and a black and then light margin. The male has distinct bars across the back (faint in *B. picta* and absent in the other species). It differs from *B. simplex*, *B. falx*, and *B. taeniata* in having yellow-gold rather than green-blue opercle scales, a narrow rather than wide distal (outer) band on the anal and caudal fins, in scale and fin ray counts, and in the relative locations of the fins.

B. picta should have clean, clear, cool (75°F [24°C]) water of neutral pH. Peaceful and social, it can be held in groups in large (40 gallon [151 L]) tanks. Massive water changes trigger mass spawning. This behavior may be an adaptation to spawning during suddenly increased stream flow in the rainy season. A couple of weeks after the mass spawning, a large cohort (a group of the same origin) of babies from many broods would be released at the same time, and their large number reduces the likelihood of predation on any individual. Analogous phenomena would be synchronous coral spawning, herd behavior in African savannah herbivores, and schooling in forage fish, all providing safety in numbers by confusing the predator. A further benefit of synchronous and periodic spawning is that it will not support a predator population requiring a continuous food supply.

The abundant fry (from many synchronous spawns) are easy to raise on *Artemia* nauplii alone, reaching adult size in half a year. It has sometimes been reported as *B. trifasciata*, a synonym of the same fish. It differs from other members of the *picta* group in having a dark red rather than blue distal (outer) band in the anal and caudal fins of the males. *B. picta* is a frequent and easy spawner that will fill all available tank space with offspring. Like an alley cat, this is the gift that keeps on giving.

Unidentified species from the Kapuas River, Borneo.

"Betta taeniata"

B. taeniata REGAN, 1910 was described from the Senah River drainage in Sarawak in northeastern Borneo. Later it was found to the south in Kalimantan in the Kapuas River and at Pontianak. It's clear that the original *B. taeniata* was a Borneo fish.

There are other reports of *"B. taeniata"* from the Bataker highlands on Sumatra, from Singapore, from

"Betta taeniata" from Kapuas River, Borneo.

Thailand, and even from Vietnam. There's a good chance that the Viet Nam fish is the newly recognized *B. prima*. A report from Johore (southern Malay Peninsula) has been questioned, but I suspect it and the Singapore fish are the same.

B. taeniata is either widely distributed or the name has been used for more than one species. We don't know the origins of the hobby fish with assurance, nor whether this name is appropriate for all stocks. On geographical distances alone, I think it almost certain that the fish from Singapore, the Malay Peninsula, and Sumatra is a new, unrecognized species that is distinct from the Borneo *B. taeniata*.

Supporting this idea (or reinforcing its great adaptability) is that *"B. taeniata"* has been reported from clear, moving streams, and from turbid ditches over sand bottoms where the water was red, probably from iron particles. Iron is associated with clays and are characteristic of soft swamp water of almost zero calcium-magnesium hardness. The conductivity of water in this habitat was low (20 mS) and the afternoon temperature high (82°F [28°C]).

This lined mouthbrooder is larger than *B. picta* at more than 3 inches (7.5 cm) and varies from unlined in nuptial coloration to three-lined on a gray to yellowish body in juveniles and in submissive dress. A dark band in the anal and caudal fins is submargined in a lighter band, but the most striking marking is the green iridescent scales on the gill cover.

In aquariums, it does best at cool temperatures (75°F [24°C]) but tolerates a variety of conditions. The female catches and spits the eggs to the male as in other mouthbrooders. Eggs number up to 300, an unusually large clutch—and a clue to which populations represent the same fish and which do not (but not to which population the true *B. taeniata* belongs). This species is not easy to keep or breed, and has never been popular. It readily succumbs to disease in fouled water. In some literature, it has been reported as *B. trifasciata* or *B. macrophthalma,* names which may have to be resurrected if indeed *"B. taeniata"* consists of more than one species. This is a perfect example of why aquarists should never mix stocks from different origins.

Betta falx

B. falx TAN AND KOTTELAT, 1998 resembles *B. picta*, which also occurs on Sumatra, but occupies a different habitat. *B. falx,* which is restricted to Sumatra, was found at the Alai River bridge near Langkat along the Muara Bungo to Muara Tebo Road, and in the Batang Hari River basin it occurs in Jambi Province and in Deli (now Medan).

This fish lives in lowland swamp forests with submerged and riparian (bank) vegetation. The water is quiet (stagnant), tinted light brown, with low to neutral pH of 4.7–6.8, low calcium-magnesium hardness of 1, and low alkaline reserve of 1. Other fishes sharing this habitat are the unnamed *Betta* sp. aff. *fusca, Parosphromenus*

Habitat of "Betta taeniata" at Sakadau; pH 5.6, DH 0, 27.7°C.

sumatranus, Sphaerichthys osphromenoides, Trichogaster trichopterus, T. leeri, Trichopsis vittata, and *Belontia hasseltii*.

Betta falx *from Jambi Province, Sumatra.*

53

B. falx is a 1.5 inch (3.5 cm) fish, small but robust, and brown with three black horizontal stripes, the central stripe longest and most distinct and originating in the snout and passing through the eye. Stripes are more prominent in juveniles, females, and the brooding male.

The nuptial male has reddish brown anal and caudal fins with a prominent light blue inner band adjacent to a black submarginal band, the fins margined in white.

In aquaria *B. falx* has no special requirements, but does best in soft, clean water with live and frozen foods and frequent water changes. It spawns near bottom in typical mouthbrooder fashion every 2 weeks, the female catching and spitting the eggs to the male, who broods until the fry are released and take live microworms or *Artemia* nauplii as first food. As for other mouthbrooders, a tank cover helps prevent jumping out, and plants and structures provide security. The best production is obtained if the brooding male is moved 3 days after spawning to a densely vegetated 10 gallon (38 L)

Habitat of **Betta simplex.**

nursery tank until he releases the fry, after which time he is removed and the fry raised in that tank.

Betta simplex

B. simplex KOTTELAT, 1994 is one of the few Thai mouthbrooder species. It was discovered at Tham Sra Kaew along National Highway 4034, a distance of 1 mile (1.5 km) northwest of Krabi in Krabi Province of southern Thailand. The habitat was the shoreline of a deep (30 feet [9 m]) pool and nine adjacent ponds in a limestone (karst) hilly area. The water was cool (72–79°F [22–26°C]), neutral (pH 7.0), with a calcium-magnesium hardness of 11 that can be attributed to seepage from the karst formations. Most of the bottom was mud and in the shallows supported *Cryptocoryne crispatula*, grasses, and hyacinth-like floating, flowering aquatic plants. Much of the open area had muddy (silted) water and vegetated shallows and shores. The general area is in a forested, limestone hill region, but the specific habitat was a wet meadow in the open full sun, the area surrounded by palm trees some distance from the water. Other *B. simplex* from karst area streams near Ao Lok were bigger, and the water harder and more basic (pH 7.5–8.0).

A robust fish with a large head and projecting lower jaw, its body is short at not more than 2 inches (10 cm) long. The male is reddish brown and the female yellowish brown. Black horizontal stripes are confined to the head, jaws, eye, and gill cover of

Betta simplex.

Betta simplex, *spawning.*

the male, but may extend the entire flank in females and juveniles. The female's unpaired fins are unmarked; those of the male are margined in a thin white line, submargined in a broad blue-black band most prominent in the anal and caudal fins, and a lighter band inward. The throat and gill cover are iridescent green in the male and mat white in the female.

B. simplex is unique among bettas in doing best at a pH near 8 and a high calcium-magnesium hardness that mimics its limestone natural habitat. You can attain these conditions by adding commercial marine aquarium kalkwasser (limewater, calcium hydroxide solution) and alkalinity supplement (sodium carbonate and sodium borate) to the water, or simply including a filter package containing aragonite gravel. Do not adjust pH with baking soda, because its effects are temporary and the pH will be unstable. A stable elevated hardness and basic pH also extend Artemia nauplii survival, so live food is available longer after feeding.

B. simplex breeds in the typical mouthbrooder manner, the female catching and spitting the eggs to the male for brooding. He releases the large fry 10 days later, when they take live *Artemia* nauplii or microworms at once. B. simplex is on the IUCN Red List because its localized distribution makes it vulnerable to extinction.

Betta edithae

B. edithae VIERKE, 1984 was described from the Barito River delta at Bandjarmasin, on Bangka Island off the southeastern coast of Sumatra, and the mainland at Palumbang. It was found in a tidal tributary of the lower Mentaya River, downstream from Sampit; in a tributary of the Sepatah River; and in a tributary of the Mandor River—all in the region of Sumatra and surrounding islands in the western Sunda Islands. Other reports of this fish include a locale about 16 miles (26 km) northeast of Pontianak in Kalimantan; in a tributary to the Keniyatan River; and in a tributary of the Landak River, about 40 miles (64 km) northeast of Pontianak and 17 miles (27 km) west of Ngabang—all locations on Borneo far to

Betta edithae *of Sumatra.*

the east of Sumatra. The habitats are reported as darkly shaded forested tributary streams or sunny pools in the open connected to larger rivers, in still or slightly flowing water 3–6 feet (1–2 m) deep. Some are black-water and others not. These differences in habitat and locality suggest at least two separate species are being reported as *B. edithae*. The name can be applied with certainty only to the Bangka Island population, the basis of the original description. I suspect the Borneo fish may be an unnamed different biological species,

Betta *sp. from Bangka Island (B. edithae?).*

even though the fish may look alike based on simple measurements and pigment patterns.

B. edithae grows to more than 3 inches (7.5 cm), but is usually smaller. Displaying males are brown with rows of iridescent green scale edges. The unpaired fins are richly hued with brown rays and light blue membranes, and there is a white submarginal band in the anal fin. A black band from the lower lips extends through the eye across the gill cover. Brooding males are lighter, with three or four black horizontal lines, the second through the eye to the lips. Females are slightly smaller, not as colorful, and have shorter unpaired fins than males.

B. edithae is a peaceful fish without rigorous water quality requirements and will spawn in a community tank. Maintain a moderate calcium-magnesium hardness of 10–20 (although this might not be important), pH of 5.0–7.5, and temperature of 77–82°F (25–28°C), with higher temperatures to induce breeding. Salt or limestone in the water enhances

Artemia longevity. The fish will spawn in or near a large flowerpot cave near the bottom or near the surface in typical mouthbrooder fashion, with an embrace and the female gathering eggs that she spits to the male for incubation. The female is ignored after breeding. If moved to a 10–20 gallon (38–76 L) densely planted tank after a few days, the male is likely to carry the eggs and fry to term. At 82°F (28°C), he releases 20–100 fry at 7–10 days, and the guppy-sized young take live *Artemia* nauplii or microworms at once. The fry should have frequent feedings and water changes of 5–10 percent every 2 days. They grow rapidly, but massive water changes sometimes induce skin irritations in the young, perhaps by diluting the protective salts. Maturity is reached at 6 months. Because of doubts about identity, stocks from different known origins should not be mixed.

Betta prima

B. prima KOTTELAT, 1994 was reported from Chanthaburi, Trot, and Sa Kaeo provinces in southeastern Thailand and from the Phnom Penh to Sihanoukville Road in Cambodia. The type locality is a creek 0.6 mile (1 km) from Chantaburi and downstream of Nam Tok Krating under the Chantabur-Trat Highway toward Nam Tok Phliu. It is also known from Klong Nakon Noi Nakon Sritamarat and near the Tha Krabak Waterfall in Thailand. It ranges at least to Kirikum, Stung Treng, Stun Tong Hong, and Sihanoukville in Cambodia.

Betta prima.

B. prima lives in small, slow-flowing streams and sunny, open, shallow marsh pools over a gravel or mud bottom at neutral pH, but has also been found near a waterfall. Silt-laden water and full sun exposure indicates considerable temperature fluctuation in nature.

The (maximum) 4 inch (10 cm) fish is distinguished by an uninterrupted lower-head stripe continuing onto the gill cover, no central ray extensions in the caudal fin, and dorsal fin rays not elongated. The body is light brown, darker above, with three dark horizontal stripes along the flank. The throat and gill cover are deep iridescent green. Rows of brown spots cross the dorsal fin, the caudal fin is colorless, and the anal fin has a narrow dark margin. It resembles the *picta* group in the margin on the anal fin, but has more rays in the anal fin and no dark margin in the caudal fin. It also breeds at an unusually small size of less than 1 inch (2.5 cm), even attaining four times that length. This mouthbrooder should have a dark-ened, covered tank and be fed mostly live foods.

Pugnax Group

The *B. pugnax* species group (*B. pugnax, B. pulchra, B. schalleri, B. breviobesus, B. enisae, B. fusca, B. lehi*) are upland fishes from flowing waters in Borneo, Sumatra, the Malay Peninsula, and Indo-China. They all have a large head, which measures 28–40 percent of the body length (from the tip of the snout to the base of the tail fin); greenish blue scales on the gill covers and often the body, throat, and belly; and an elongate, lance-shaped caudal fin with concentric dark rings in the males of some but not all species.

Betta pugnax

B. pugnax CANTOR, 1849 was redescribed by Tan and Tan (1996) and ranges from southern Thailand southward through the Malay Penin-sula to its offshore islands. Popu-lations have been found in the

Betta pugnax.

Terenggannu, Pahang, Perak, Selan-gor, and Johor Provinces, on Penang Island off Kedah Province, and on Singapore at the southern tip of the peninsula. (*Betta bleekeri* is an invalid synonym of *B. pugnax*.) The fish cir-culating in the hobby as *Betta* cf. *pugnax* "Nanga Tayap" has not been evaluated and might be a separate species.

B. pugnax is slender and large, and can attain 5 inches (12.5 cm). The body is dark brown with bluish green iridescent scales on the gill covers, and sometimes on the throat and abdomen. Juveniles and females have two horizontal stripes forward from a basicaudal spot to join two stripes on the side of the head. Adults have elongated and broadly lance-shaped caudal fins. The male has deeper color, a slightly longer anal fin, and indistinct dark concen-tric bars in the caudal fin.

It lives in hill country rivers and streams with clear, cool water, neutral to slightly alkaline pH (7.1–7.5), flow-ing over sandy or rubble bottoms. It avoids the current and occurs along shorelines and in backwaters among vegetation and leaf litter, but some-times even near waterfalls.

A pair or trio (one male and two females) should have a large (not less than 20 gallons [76 L]), covered, well-vegetated tank with flowerpot caves or 3 inch (7.5 cm) diameter PVC tube hiding places, and high-quality, cool (70–75°F [21–24°C]), well-aerated, and frequently changed (25 percent per week) water. An out-side power filter with a carbon cartridge helps with current and aeration. Cover the sides and back of the tank with black plastic, and provide duckweed or other floating plants for the surface. This shading induces the male to intensify his color. All foods are greedily taken, including flakes and pellets, but mixed frozen foods (brine shrimp, bloodworms, mysids), live black worms, and especially chopped earthworms provide optimal nutrition. Spawning is in typical mouthbrooder fashion, near the bottom in a clearing, with the female catching and spitting the eggs to the male. He should be moved 3 days later to a densely vegetated 20 gallon (76 L) tank to incubate and finally release the fry. From 40–100 baby guppy-sized fry take *Artemia* nauplii and microworms upon release less than 2 weeks later, and are half grown in 6 months if provided frequent partial water changes

Betta *cf.* pugnax *from Nanga Sayap.*

Betta pulchra

B. *pulchra* TAN AND TAN, 1996 differs from B. *pugnax* in having a narrowly lance-shaped caudal fin, a more robust body, greater distribution of greenish blue rather than bluish green iridescent scales extending over the flanks, dark concentric or ladder-like marks on the dorsal fin but *not* the caudal, and red and black margins on the anal fin. Even the edges of the pelvic (ventral) fins are iridescent green. It is only slightly smaller than B. *pugnax*, at 4 inches (10 cm).

B. *pulchra* was first reported from Kampong Jasa Sepakat, Pontian, in Johore on the southwestern side of the Malay Peninsula, and has since been caught elsewhere in Johore.

It occurs in densely overgrown blackwater irrigation canals at a pH of 3.9–4.2, and initially was thought to be a blackwater phenotype of B. *pugnax*. However, when offspring of the two species were grown in both kinds of water, they bred true to their parental types. Associates of B. *pulchra* include *Belontia hasselti, Sphaerichthys osphromenoides, Parosphromenus* sp., *Trichopsis vittata, Betta bellica,* and B. *imbellis*. It

Betta pulchra *from Pontian, Sumatra.*

59

Long-fin **Betta splendens.**

Betta pulchra *from Pontian, Sumatra.*

Betta breviobesus *from Kapuas River, Borneo.*

is never found with *B. pugnax*, which does not occur in this type of habitat.

There is little information on the fish, although it is common and not demanding. Provide a covered, darkened, densely vegetated aquarium of at least 20 gallons (76 L). Java moss (*Vesicularia*) and many *Cryptocoryne* species withstand low light, and water sprite (*Ceratopteris*) or duckweed (*Lemna*) on the brightly lit surface provide shading. Feed frozen and live foods only. Keep the pH low and the water quality high with frequent partial water changes. Spawning behavior is similar to *B. pugnax*.

Betta breviobesus

B. breviobesus TAN AND KOTTELAT, 1998 was described from a tributary of the middle Kapuas River 54 miles (87 km) east of Pontianak, and 0.6 mile (1 km) up the Tajan River from Tajan, in West Kalimantan on Borneo. The specimens were caught in traps to collect baitfish in small forest streams of neutral to slightly acidic pH (6.0–7.0).

This 2.5 inch (6.5 cm) fish lacks a dark chin bar (found in *B. pugnax, B. pulchra,* and *B. prima*), and has dark margins on the caudal and anal fins (lacking in *B. pugnax, B. fusca, B. pulchra, B. prima*, and *B. schalleri*).

Betta enisae

B. enisae KOTTELAT, 1995 was discovered in tributaries of the Santik River and in a tributary of the Towang River, in the Kapuas River system of Kalimantan on Borneo.

It occurred in leaf litter in a shallow forest stream. The water was cool, slightly acidic (pH 5.5–6.0), and soft (calcium-magnesium hardness 10, alkalinity 1).

It's an active fish, up to 4.5 inches (11 cm) long (females slightly smaller), dark gray-brown, with a sharply pointed (lanceolate) caudal fin, iridescent blue-green scales on the lower gill covers and throat, a black stripe through the eye, and black-edged caudal and anal fins with spectacular broad and bright blue submargins that are characteristic of the species. The coloration of the male intensifies during courtship.

Provide a 30 gallon (114 L) covered tank with the sides and back darkened with black plastic; abundant vegetation everywhere, including water sprite or duckweed on the surface; hiding places for the female; clean water at pH 6.0–7.2; and a temperature of 75–79°F (24–26°C). Calcium-magnesium hardness seems unimportant. Use an outside power filter with carbon filtration to maintain water quality, and add hardwood leaves for acidification. Feed heavily and often with frozen and live foods. Heavy feedings cause a great deal of waste and must be countered with frequent massive water changes to maintain water quality. *B. enisae* spawns near the bottom in typical mouthbrooder fashion, with the female recovering first from the spawning embrace and gathering eggs that she spits toward the male. He catches and incubates them for about 10 days before releasing about 100 fry. Unlike other mouthbrooders, the male's buccal cavity does not

Betta enisae, *spawning.*

swell greatly, and he feeds during incubation. For maximum production, move the incubating male to a well-vegetated grow-out tank. The fry graze on the attached microbes in the vegetation, but also take microworms and live *Artemia* nauplii right away. Maturity is reached in 6 months.

Betta schalleri

B. schalleri KOTTELAT AND NG, 1994 was described from Bangka Island off the southeast coast of Sumatra, along the road between Pangkalpinang and Payung, at Tobaoli and Mentok; and in the Mangong Forest Reserve near Petingdang between Desa Kurau and Desa Balilik. The original location was 3.3 miles (5.5 km) north of Payung on the road to Pangkalpinang. I suspect that reports of it in Kalimantan, Borneo, are of another species.

It occurs in swamps, forest streams, and hill streams, in soft, lightly tanned water of pH 4.5–5.5, calcium-magnesium hardness of 1,

Electron microscope photo of Betta fusca *egg.*

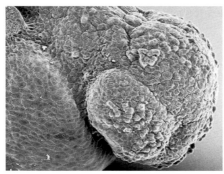

Electron microscope photo of Betta fusca, *head of larva.*

alkalinity of 1, and temperature of 83°F (28°C).

This 4.5 inch (11 cm) mouth-brooder is gray to brown with large green scales on most of the gill covers and throat, and with finely green-edged scales on the body, forming indistinct rows of light spots. Females and males out of breeding color have three horizontal black stripes along the flank, the central stripe most prominent. The boldest character is the marking of the anal fin, a broad white deeply submarginal band bordered outside with a thin black band, and finally a thin white marginal band. The male's unpaired fins are slightly more elongated than the female's, and there is a dark band from the tip of the nose to the end of the green-scaled gill cover.

Keep a pair in a shaded 20 gallon (76 L) aquarium (or larger), with good filtration and frequent water changes. Water quality parameters are pH 5.8–6.5, temperature 71–77°F (22–25°C), calcium-magnesium hardness of 1 or 2, and alkalinity of 1. Live and frozen food recommended.

Betta fusca

B. fusca REGAN, 1910 was described from Singkek, near Pakanbaru, on the west coast of central Sumatra. In 1993 Kottelat and associates also reported it from Sumatra and across the Melaka Strait on the Malay Peninsula. Malay Peninsula localities include Teloh Bahang, on Penang Island off the northwest coast of the peninsula just south of Thailand, and mainland sites at the Mertang River near Kual Pilah, Temerloh in Perak, and at Terachi. Sumatra is split by a volcanic mountain range, and it is curious that this fish occurs on both sides of the range.

The habitat was pH 5.5–7.0, calcium-magnesium hardness 12, and temperature of 72–79°F (22–26°C). A photograph from a Web site shows a small, fast flowing, clear, slightly tinted forest stream with patchy vegetation over a dark bottom, shaded by overhanging trees and shrubs, and the bank soil a mix of gravel with mostly sandy mud. A breeding report from the Web reports the fish as imported from Borneo. Assuming we can discount this error, other information indicates a fish richly adorned with iridescent green scales, mostly on the gill covers and throat. This purported *Betta fusca* spawned in typical mouthbrooder fashion, with the fry released after 2 weeks.

Betta lehi

B. lehi from Sarawak is the most recently (possibly) introduced member to the *pugnax* group, and the technical information had not arrived at press time. Because of premature release of this name without an accompanying description, it may be withdrawn as a proposed species name.

Waseri Group

The *B. waseri* group (*B. waseri, B. tomi, B. spilotogena, B. pi, B. renata, B. hipposideros, B. anabatoides, B. chloropharynx*) are called the big yellow mouthbrooders. Many are moderately large (2.5 inch [6 cm] body length exclusive of the tail fin), with yellow-brown bodies, and with iridescent gold scales on the flanks. The most striking character is a golden iris divided into two concentric rings by a thin red line.

Each species within the group has distinctive black markings on the

Markings of species in the waseri group.

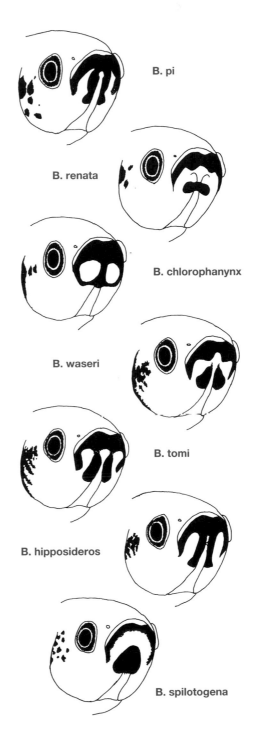

B. pi

B. renata

B. chlorophanynx

B. waseri

B. tomi

B. hipposideros

B. spilotogena

Betta waseri *from Pahang.*

lower face and chin. They also share a long body stripe from the eye to the tail spot, and a shorter secondary stripe just above the anal fin.

Members of the mouthbrooding *waseri* group live in ancient peat swamp forests, just like the bubble-nesters of the *coccina* group. The *waseri* group ranges from southern Thailand and the Malay Peninsula, across the Melaka Strait to Sumatra and Bangka Island and islands of the Riau Archipelago off eastern Sumatra. There are also two reports from Borneo, in similar swamp forest habitat.

Like the bubblenesting *coccina* group, the mouthbrooding *waseri* group is ecologically specialized to occupy stenotopic shallow, blackwaters in forested peat swamps. These blackwater, leaf-littered conditions are easily duplicated in aquaria. The fish are tolerant of hard water and not as dependent on low pH, but creating those conditions (RO water, dried hardwood leaves, peat moss, dense vegetation) increases the chances of breeding. Many of our popular aquar-

ium fishes normally kept in neutral water, such as blue and pearl gouramies (*Trichogaster*), are also found in these extremely acidic habitats along with such acid-loving blackwater fishes as the licorice gouramies (*Parosphromenus*).

Betta waseri

B. waseri KRUMMENACHER, 1986 was described from two locations on the Malay Peninsula, Pahang in the Kuantan area and a second site 20 miles (32 km) north toward Pekam. The Kuantan site was destroyed by encroaching development, which remains the greatest threat to many forest species of *Betta*.

The fish lives amid dense layers of leaf litter and riparian tree roots and other vegetation in shaded blackwater forest streams where the bottom is mud and the water soft and acidic (pH 4.0–5.0). Other anabantoids in this habitat include *Betta bellica, B. tussyae, Parosphromenus nagyi, Sphaerichthys osphromenoides, Trichogaster trichopterus* and *Belontia hasselti*.

This 4 inch (10 cm) yellowish gray mouthbrooder has a black lower jaw and a pair of teardrop-shaped black chin marks.

B. waseri requires a large surface area but little depth. A half-filled 30 gallon (114 L) tank is suitable. The tank should be densely vegetated and have abundant twigs, a flowerpot, and PVC pipe caves for security. Darken the back and sides of the tank with black plastic. Fill with RO water, and provide leaves for tannic and humic acid extraction to lower the pH and stain the water for inducing spawning. Neutral, unstained, hard water is tolerated. Live and frozen foods should comprise the diet. Spawning occurs near the bottom, with the female picking up the eggs and spitting them to the male for incubation. The large fry (about 100) can take *Artemia* nauplii and microworms as first food. The fish circulating in the hobby as *Betta* sp. aff. *waseri* "Pekam Nanas" might be from Pekam, but should be considered of uncertain taxonomic position.

Betta tomi *from Kota Tingii.*

Betta tomi

B. tomi NG AND KOTTELAT, 1994 was described from a site along the road from Kota Tingii to Mersind in eastern Johore in the south of the Malay Peninsula, and might once have occurred at the tip of the peninsula at Singapore. The fish circulating in the hobby as *Betta* sp. aff. *tomi* "Sungai Penjuh, Anjungen" is of uncertain taxonomic position. The Penjuh River is across the Strait of Melaka at the east end of Sumatra, and Anjungen is on Borneo, outside the range of this group.

The habitat at Johore is a shallow, shaded, blackwater swamp forest tributary of the Mupor River with a pH of 5.5. The bottom is deep, soft mud, littered with leaves and twigs. Other anabantoids in this stream were *Trichogaster trichopterus* and *Betta pulchra* (reported as *B. pugnax*).

This short, thick-bodied fish has two oval black spots on the chin that do not connect to the lower jaw. The male has a wide dark green band on the anal fin, and is reddish brown with a lighter chest. The black stripe on the flank is doubled, with black spots below. Because of threats to its habitat and apparent extirpation (local extinction) from Singapore, it is on the IUCN Red List of vulnerable species.

Betta renata

B. renata TAN, 1998 was collected from Rantau Panjang and Pematang Lumut in Jambi Province, Sumatra. It was found near a rubber plantation in a previously logged peat forest blackwater swamp at low pH (4.1) commonly harvested for aquarium fishes. In the same waters were *Rasbora*

Betta renata *from Sumatra.*

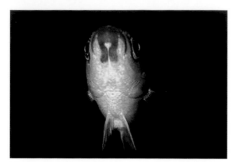

Betta pi, *chin markings.*

Betta pi, *male.*

kalochroma, Betta coccina, B. simorum, Sphaerichthys osphromenoides, Nandus nebulosus, Belontia hasselti, Puntius hexazona, Mystus bimaculatus, Clarias teijsmanni, Kottelatlimia pristes (a cobitid), and other fishes.

This is the same fish that Weber & De Beaufort incorrectly identified as

Betta spilotogena *from Bintan Island.*

B. anabatoides in 1922. It has a kidney-shaped black throat marking not connected to a black lower jaw. There is no black margin on the anal fin, but there is a black margin on the lower edge of the gill cover. At 5.5 inches (14 cm), it is one of the largest mouthbrooders.

Betta pi

B. pi TAN, 1998, the northernmost member of the B. waseri group, was collected in an unshaded open area in a logged peat swamp forest floodplain 3.5 miles (9 km) north of the Kolok River at Mae Nam Tod Deng, Narathiwat Province, and at 7 miles (11 km) southwest of Tak Bai in southern Thailand (northern Malay Peninsula).

The water was soft, not very acidic at pH 6.0, and up to 4 feet (1 m) deep over a soft mud bottom, but was not or at least was no longer a blackwater habitat. The only other fishes were Channa lucius and Parosphromenus cf. paludicola.

The black pigment on the jaw is the same width as and is contiguous with the black edging on the beginning of each lower gill plate, providing the illusion of a black Greek letter pi. The anal fin of adults has a thin dark blue edge. This fish is on the IUCN Red List of threatened species. No breeding information at present.

Betta spilotogena

B. spilotogena NG AND KOTTELAT, 1994 is known from Bintan Island, in the Riau Island Archipelago just east of Singapore. On the north end of Bintan, it was collected in shaded,

shallow (3 feet [1 m]), densely vegetated, blackwater swamp streams
and backwaters at pH 4.9–5.5.

This mouthbrooder has two wide
oval spots barely touching one
another on the throat, but that do
not reach up to the lower jaw. The
body is brown with scattered gold-
edged scales, and the unpaired fins
are blue-purple with brown margins.
The fish is on the IUCN Red List of
threatened species.

It breeds as a typical mouthbrooder and produces up to 180 fry
that, at 0.25 inch (0.6 cm), can take
brine shrimp nauplii or microworms
at once.

Betta hipposideros *from north Selangor.*

Betta hipposideros

B. hipposideros NG AND KOTTELAT,
1994 was discovered at North
Selangor on the Malay Peninsula
between the Besar River and Tanjun
Malim at the 24 mile (39 km) marker,
and at Perak.

It lives in shallow streams and
pools of leaf-littered, blackwater,
highly acidic (pH 3.5–3.7) peat forest
swamps. Other anabantoids in these
waters are *Betta bellica, B. livida,
Parosphromenus harveyi,* Sphaerichthys osphromenoides, Trichogaster leeri, T. pectoralis, T. trichopterus,* and *Belontia hasselti.*

This fish has horseshoe-shaped
chin markings, and dark bars on the
caudal fin. It is on the IUCN Red List
of vulnerable species.

Betta anabatoides

B. anabatoides BLEEKER, 1850 was
originally described from Banjar-
masin, in South Kalimantan, Borneo.

It has also been reported from 5
miles (8 km) miles north of Kota
Tinggi in a small forested stream
flowing into the main stem of
the Melawi River (in the Serundung
River basin) about 1 mile (1.5 km)
upstream of Fromnangapino.
Another report is from Bunguran
Island in East Kalimantan about 20
miles (32 km) northwest of Balikpapan, in a muddy seepage pool in a
dry stream bed of the Kapuas River
basin in Central Kalimantan. There is
one report from Sumatra, which
should be held in doubt because of
the distance and isolation from the
general range of the fish. There are
fish in the hobby labeled *Betta* cf.

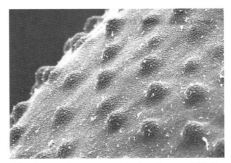
Electron microscope photo of egg of Betta
anabatoides.

Betta chloropharynx, *pair from Koba, Bangka Island.*

anabatoides, probably from unknown locales or otherwise not originating with scientists.

Linke described the habitat as clear, slightly tinted water with pH 4.8 or less and low conductivity (27–30 mS). The fish occurred in dense, bankside vegetation. A habitat photo by Hiroyuki Kishi (Team Borneo) shows a small, blackwater, almost stagnant creek with steep banks shaded by overhanging trees. It was found together with the smaller *Betta edithae*.

Males may have blue-green iridescent scales on the body and a hint of yellow in the anal fin. Females have no bright colors or yellow in the anal fin, but both sexes may have fringed, spade-shaped caudal fins. It's a large fish, at 5 inches (12.5 cm).

In aquaria it spawned at 75–80°F (24–26.5°C). It is not colorful and not widely kept. Size dictates it should have a 20–30 gallon (76–114 L) aquarium.

Betta chloropharynx

B. chloropharynx KOTTELAT AND NG, 1994 was collected at the 60 mile (97 km) marker south of Pangkalpinang on the road to Toboali, and 25.5 miles (41 km) south of Koba, on Bangka Island off the southeast coast of Sumatra.

The blackwater swamp habitat was the leaf litter in a shallow pool in a clear, blackish brown creek in secondary growth forest. The water was pH 4.8, calcium-magnesium hardness 0–1, and alkalinity 0–1.

B. chloropharynx exceeds 4 inches (10 cm) in length, and has large chin ocelli of black circles surrounding iridescent green inclusions. The caudal fin is rhomboid to slightly lanceolate, the body yellowish brown, darker above, with light spotting on the lower flank, and an iridescent golden spot adorns the gill cover. A broad light band in the middle of the flank splits the fish into two dark and two light stripes. The

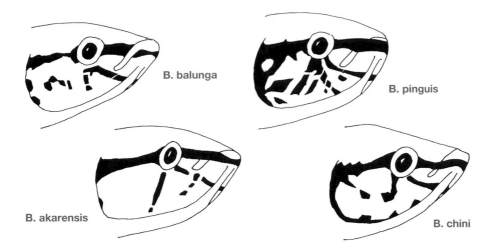

B. balunga

B. pinguis

B. akarensis

B. chini

Markings of species in the akarensis group.

fish is on the IUCN Red List of vulnerable species.

Akarensis **Group**

The *B. akarensis* species group (*B. akarensis, B. balunga, B. chini, B. pinguis*, and perhaps two other unnamed species) is restricted to Borneo. Members have a black stripe on the cheek from the tip of the snout to the eye, another complete lower stripe, and a stripe from behind the eye (postorbital) to the gill opening. There are no iridescent scales on the gill covers. The caudal fin is rhomboidal rather than rounded, and has concentric dark markings in the membranes.

Betta akarensis

B. akarensis REGAN, 1910 was described from a single juvenile specimen from the Akar River in central Sarawak in the north of Borneo. Vierke's (1984) *Betta climacura* is a synonym. Vierke found it at Rampayoh in northern Sarawak, and Linke found it in the Sekerang River around Bandar Sri Aman in western Sarawak. *Betta akarensis* dwells among and beneath dense shoreline vegetation in small streams with fast-flowing water.

B. akarensis varies from dark gray without stripes to light gray with three black stripes, the middle one passing through the eye to the lips, and the lines separated by horizontal rows of black spots. Each pair of black stripes with its included row of black spots may darken to form a wide black horizontal band. Males have elongated unpaired fins, but no striking colors. This is a large fish, attaining 5.5 inches (14 cm).

A pair should have a 20 gallon (80 L) covered tank with blackened sides and back, abundant vegeta-

Betta akarensis.

Spawning clasp of Betta akarensis.

Male Betta balunga.

tion and hiding places, and cool (68–77°F [20–25°C]), slightly acidic (pH 5.0–6.8), soft (hardness 7–12), alkaline (0–4) water. Provide flow with a small power head, sponge filter, or an outside power filter, and stain and acidify the water with hardwood leaves. *B. akarensis* does well on a diet of mixed live foods (including chopped earthworms) and frozen foods.

The female initiates breeding, repeatedly bumping the male and leading him to a clearing in the vegetation. They spawn near the bottom, and the female gathers and spits the eggs to the male for incubation. Up to 30 eggs 1.2 mm in diameter are expelled at each embrace. Incubation takes 12–15 days, after which he orients vertically and expels about 10 fry at a time. The young are 0.25 inch (0.6 cm) long, may number more than 100, and take *Artemia* nauplii at once. Moving the male 2 days after spawning to a 20–40 gallon (76–156 L) grow-out tank will increase the odds that he carries to term. After fry release, change 25 percent of the grow-out tank water weekly.

Betta balunga

B. balunga HERRE, 1940 is native to a small, high gradient stream in the Balung River drainage, part of the Sebuku River system in Sabah, eastern Malaysia, in the north of Borneo. It was found 45 miles (72 km) from Tawau, and at East Tawau Semborna, 20 miles (32 km) east of Tawau.

This robust 5 inch (12.5 cm) mouthbrooder (females are a bit smaller) is dark gray with blue highlights in the anal fin and sometimes the lower caudal. A broad black line from the lips through the eye crosses the gill plates and continues to a basicaudal spot near the base of the tail. The band may fade behind the gill covers. The male's caudal fin has a netlike pigment pattern and the central rays extend beyond the fin. The anal fin is dark margined with a white submarginal band. In nuptial coloration, the male develops a dark mask, a second black line extends downward from the eye, and the iris becomes red. The nuptial female lightens, and develops a dark band on the back and another in the midline of the flank.

In an unpublished Web report, Jan Rehwinkel and Christian Redweik recommended a covered 20 gallon (76 L) tank with a thick layer of surface plants to diffuse the light, and abundant rooted or attached plants that require little light, such as *Cryptocoryne affinis* and Java fern. The fish are not choosy about food, and do well on mosquito larvae, daphnia, brine shrimp, and fruit flies. Adjust the water to pH 5.2–7.0, calcium-magnesium hardness of 10, and a temperature of 70–80°F (21–27°C). Provide a filter to supply current and maintain water quality.

The fish breed when two-thirds grown, usually spawning in a cave (PVC pipe, flowerpot), and sometimes near the surface. After considerable foreplay, they finally succeed with protracted embraces that produce eggs. The male bends tightly during mating, perhaps to protect eggs from being swept by a current. The female gathers and spits several at a time to the male. Afterward, she ignores him and he stays near the surface among plants. Some males will eat the eggs. Rehwinkel and Redweik noted that a disturbed male may spit out the eggs or fry, and prefer not to move him to a grow-out tank until just days before the end of the 2-week incubation period. Up to 100 fry are produced per spawn, and are easily raised after starting them on live brine shrimp nauplii or microworms.

Betta chini

B. chini NG, 1993 was discovered along the road between Beaufort and Kota Kinabalu, in eastern Sabah in North Borneo. Independently, in March 1993, Phil Dickman (who discussed this fish in *Der Makropode* as an unnamed species related to *B. akarensis*) found it on the road from Sipitang to Mesapol, also in Sabah.

Both locations are peat swamps near the coast, where almost all the original forest had been removed. The small, remnant blackwater biotopes may be all that is left of its natural range. Dickman's fish were in a blackwater drain from a plantation that emptied to a natural blackwater stream. The bottom was clay, covered with branches, twigs, and leaves, and the drain was shaded by riparian trees its entire course. The water was motionless at the time, dark as coffee,

Female **Betta chini.**

the temperature 80°F (26.5°C), the pH 4.5–5.0, and the calcium-magnesium hardness less than 3. Other fish found in these waters were *Rasbora einthovenii baramensis, Paraluciosoma sumatrana, Trichopterus trichopterus, Luciocephalus pulcher,* and the catfish *Ompok.*

This 4 inch (10 cm) fish has dark scales with iridescent light blue-white edges, a black stripe through the lips, eyes, and gill cover, a broad black mark under the chin, and a bold black stripe behind the eye and extending to the lower base of the tail fin; above this stripe is a narrower but equally conspicuous stripe running from behind the gill cover to the upper base of the tail. All the fins have white margins. Both sexes have lightly spotted unpaired fins, but those of the male are longer. During courtship, the female becomes dark above and light below, with two dark horizontal stripes. The male's color intensifies, his head becomes almost

black, his body dark brown, and his fins deep wine red.

Despite the high acidity of its natural habitat, Dickman's fish did not thrive in an acidic tank. *Betta chini* should be kept in a 20 gallon (76 L) tank with slightly acidic water (pH 5.5–6.5) darkened with hardwood leaves. Add surface and rooted vegetation for shade and security. Dickman's fish developed head infections, which he attributed to the strongly acidic water, but that is probably incorrect. Because he fed dried and flake foods, I suspect leftover decayed foods degraded the water quality and sickened his fish. Always feed live or frozen foods, even if all you have are newly hatched *Artemia* nauplii and frozen adults or frozen bloodworms. I never feed dried foods to bettas precisely because they often cause pollution that weakens the fish and makes them susceptible to infections.

In good health, spawning is preceded by hours of false starts on the day before spawning. Successful spawning can last all the next day. The female spits the eggs to the male for incubation, and may play with them if he is not fast enough. The fry hatch within 3 days, but inexperienced males may eat the first spawns. With experience, the male holds them to term, almost 2 weeks. The 40–50 fry are 0.25 inches (0.6 cm) long and take live *Artemia* nauplii at once. Dickman remarked that his three pairs, all in different aquaria, always spawned on the same day and suspected communication, but more likely they were responding to common stimuli.

Betta pinguis

B. pinguis TAN AND KOTTELAT, 1998 was collected from the Letang River, near Kampung Kandung Suli (Kecamatan Jongkong) in the middle Kapuas River basin of West Kalimantan, Borneo. No habitat information is available.

The type specimens were caught by fishermen in a small blackwater stream on hook and line among large numbers of *Betta enisae* and smaller numbers of *B. dimidiata* being captured as bait for a notopterid.

This 3.5 inch (9 cm) betta is the most deep bodied of the *akarensis* group, and has the most densely pigmented gill cover. It differs from others of the group in scale and fin ray counts (meristics), but is not otherwise remarkable. It is light brown all over, with a white band above the lateral line about three scale rows wide. A black stripe reaches from the lower jaw through the eye to the edge of the gill plate. The unpaired fins are edged in white, and the anal fin rays are extended in the male, whose caudal fin is spade shaped. No aquarium information is available.

Foerschi Group

The *Betta foerschi* species group contains at least four beautiful species (*B. foerschi, B. strohi, B. rubra,* and an unnamed species) characterized by a dark body and

Betta foerschi.

two orange bars on the gill covers of the male.

Betta foerschi

B. foerschi VIERKE, 1979 was described from the Mantaya (Metaya) River system, 150 miles (241 km) northwest of Bandjarmasin, and has also been reported from the Kahajan and Sampit River drainages. So far it has been found near Mandor, Kubu, Pudakuali, Tankaling, Tarantang, and Tumbantiti, all in Kalimantan. Fishes from different origins should be kept separately, because they may not all be the same species. For example, *Betta strohi* SCHALLER AND KOTTELAT, 1989 was described from Nataik Sedawak, about 20 miles (32 km) south of Sukamara, and from Nippa and Palangan, in the Jelai and Bila River basins in Kalimantan, and it's possible that *B. strohi* is a synonym of *B. foerschi*. It was reported as *B.* sp. from Tarantang, and illustrated in Linke (1991). The reported differences between the two "species" is slight and not, to my mind, convincing.

B. foerschi was found among fallen leaves at the bottom of a shallow swamp forest pool at Mandor. The water was pH 4.6–5.5, calcium-magnesium hardness 0–1, alkalinity 0–1, conductivity 75 mS, temperature 77–79°F (25–26°C), and color clear and deep black.

It attains 1.5 inches (4 cm) in length, plus the tail fin. The male is reddish brown above, and iridescent green on his flanks, the green extending into the spade-shaped caudal fin. The pelvic and anal fins are indigo blue, and the dorsal fin is brown. Each gill cover has two spectacular vertical yellow-orange bars separated by a black bar. The iris is iridescent. The female is brown with seven indistinct black bars extending from the base of the anal fin into the lower two-thirds of the flank, some black on the caudal fin, and her fins generally are reddish.

B. foerschi should have a covered 20 gallon (76 L) tank with RO water, floating and planted vegetation, peat moss and dried hardwood leaves to leach tannins and lower the pH to 4.5–5.0, frequent small water changes, and live foods only. It spawns near the bottom. The male

Wild Betta "strohi."

may pick up the eggs himself or the female will pick them up and spit them to him. Incubation is about 2 weeks. Each spawn produces about 40 black fry, 0.25–0.33 inch (0.6–0.7 cm) long, that take newly hatched brine shrimp at once.

Betta rubra

Little was known of *B. rubra* PERUGIA, 1893, and for many years aquarists thought it might have been a misnamed red form of *Betta splendens*, but that isn't possible. It was originally reported from Lake Toba on Sumatra (where *B. splendens* does not occur) more than a hundred years ago. In the past decade, it was collected again and specimens deposited in the Hamburg Museum and the British Museum. Recently, scientists at the University of Singapore resurrected it as a valid species, and determined it is a mouthbrooder in the *foerschi* group. At this writing it is not yet in the hobby and has not been formally redescribed.

Albimarginata Group

Among the most beautiful mouthbrooders are the *albimarginata* group consisting of *B. albimarginata* and *B. channoides* from Kalimantan, Borneo. Both have wide flat heads, and a dorsal fin insertion (the location of the first ray) only slightly behind the insertion of the first anal fin rays. Both differ from other *Betta* species by more spines in the anal fin (9–12 versus 0–4) and fewer soft (articulated) rays (11–13 versus 18–32). A third population was found in the Sesayap River basin in far north Kalimantan. This one has wide white margins on its unpaired fins. A fourth population (or species) was collected in the lower Mahakam River basin around Panpang, in central Kalimantan. The identity of these fishes has not been established, and they might yet be found to represent four (or more) distinct species. For this reason, stocks that reach the hobby should be kept separated to avoid inadvertently producing hybrids.

Betta albimarginata

B. albimarginata KOTTELAT AND NG, 1994 was first described from the Sanul River tributary of the Tikung River in the Sebuku River drainage of East Kalimantan, Borneo. Those specimens did not survive. A later collection by Dickman, Knorr, and Grams at Malinau found them in a 6 foot (2 m) wide and 4 foot (1 m) deep, clear tributary of the Sembuak River, 62 miles (100 km) to the south. Those fish were brought into the hobby, and were discussed by Jesper Thorup and Michael Schleuter (*www.ibc-smp.org/spawn_log.html*). A fish called *Betta* cf. *albimarginata* from Pampang, found 0.6 mile (1 km) from Pampang City, appears to be the same species. Frank Schäfer's *Aqualog* book (which no betta enthusiast should be without) has photographs of stocks from several locales.

Male Betta albimarginata.

The small stream at Malinau was shaded by overhanging trees. The fish occurred near the bank in shallows 2–4 inches (5–10 cm) deep, among plant roots and leaf litter. The water was pH 5.5–6.0, calcium-magnesium hardness no more than 3, and the temperature 81°F (27°C). The current was moderate.

The flanks of *B. albimarginata* are yellowish brown to reddish brown, and the back and top of the head yellow to white with black spots. All fins except the clear pectorals are red with a broad white margin and a black submargin, a unique character of the species.

Even though not a large fish, keeping a pair or small group in a larger tank (15–20 gallon [57–76 L] for a pair or trio) is recommended because the increased water volume lowers the risk of water quality degradation from pollution. Cover the top with glass, and the sides and back with black plastic. If there is more than one male in the tank, only the dominant male will spawn. The water should be soft (RO or DI),

Male **Betta albimarginata** *brooding eggs.*

acidic (pH 5.5), and darkly stained with peat moss and tannins from dried and soaked hardwood leaves and twigs. Provide floating (water sprite, duckweed) and submersed (Java moss, Java fern, *Crypto-coryne*) vegetation, and add drift-wood and a flowerpot as territory markers and hiding places. Gently aerate with a sponge filter, and change 1–2 gallons (4–7.5 L) of water a week. Feed live daphnia, *Artemia* nauplii, white worms, grindal worms, black worms, and fruit flies, supple-mented with light feedings of frozen adult brine shrimp and bloodworms. Do not feed them dried food.

Spawning occurs near the bot-tom, with the female gathering and spitting the eggs to the male. The male's nuptial colors are now a blaz-ing black and orange. Spawning may last half a day. The eggs hatch in less than 2 weeks. Midway in the incubation period, move the male to a livebearer breeding trap hung on a densely planted grow-out tank. At release, the 0.25 inch (0.5 cm) fry are

black, and leave the bottom of the breeding trap just like baby guppies.

Use a flashlight to examine the young for velvet disease (*Piscinoo-dinium*), which can break out if the tank is not scrupulously clean. Daily siphon dead food from the bottom and keep snails, live daphnia, or freshwater shrimp in the tank as scavengers. As the fry grow, remove the larger males to other tanks or individual gallon jars. Large males inhibit submissive smaller males from showing their colors.

B. channoides

B. channoides KOTTELAT AND NG, 1994 was collected from a small, swift, brown, acidic forest stream in the Behernas River system in the middle Mahakam River basin north of Mujab (=Mujub) and Muarapahu, in South Kalimantan, Borneo. The fish were near the shoreline in leaf litter and plant roots.

At 2 inches (5 cm), it differs from *B. albimarginata* by 1 more anal spine (12), 1 or 2 more anal rays (23–25), and smaller and more numerous scales. Michael Schleuter reported that the fry are gray, whereas those of *B. albimarginata* are black. Preserved juveniles from the original collection had a pale (probably yellowish white) top of the head and back, and spotting on the fins. Preserved fish of both species could readily be distinguished by markings and morphological differ-ences. Adults of both species are drab out of spawning mode, but intensely colored in nuptial dress.

There are no obvious differences to the naked eye, so record the origin of your fish, because there are at least two other populations in this species group whose disposition is not settled.

Patoti–Unimaculata Group

The *patoti-unimaculata* group (*B. patoti, B. unimaculata, B. ocellata, B. macrostoma,* and two to four unnamed species) occurs in Kalimantan, Borneo. The adults have pointed fins, the body may be plain, spotted, or covered with iridescent scales, and the caudal of the male may be spade shaped.

Betta patoti

B. patoti WEBER AND DE BEAUFORT, 1922 was discovered near Balikpapan, in the Mangar River drainage, 15.5 miles (25 km) east of Balikpapan Bay in East Kalimantan. The photograph in Schäfer's *Aqualog* said to be from Timur (South Kalimantan) is a misidentification of *B. unimaculata.*

B. patoti does resemble *B. unimaculata,* but lacks iridescent scales on top of the head. This 4.5 inch (11 cm) fish has a large head and large eyes, and is distinct in having up to 11 dark bars on a slender body that is normally brown with a light horizontal stripe. The male has iridescent green scales on the lower body and face, and spots of red around the lips. In nuptial coloration, the female becomes lighter below with a horizontal series of black blotches, but at other times is brown. When brooding, the male reverts to light brown, sometimes with iridescent green on the top of the head.

In its native habitat, the water was measured at pH 5.5–6.8, calcium-magnesium hardness 10, and temperature 74–83°F (23–28°C).

Like other mouthbrooders, *B. patoti* should have a 20 gallon (76 L) covered aquarium with abundant vegetation everywhere and structure on the bottom. Maintain the water at pH 7.0, calcium-magnesium hardness 6, alkalinity 2, and temperature 75°F (24°C). It spawns in typical mouthbrooder fashion, and the female protects the territory during spawning.

Other *"patoti"* Populations

Betta cf. *patoti* "Turekai" looks like *B. patoti* but may be something else. Males have bright blue unpaired fins and jaws, black markings on the throat, and dark bodies with about eight vertical blue-black blotches on the lower flanks, and some red

Betta patoti.

Betta unimaculata, *male.*

below the eyes. Females are reddish brown, with some blue on the anal fin. I have been unable to identify the original location of this stock.

Schäfer illustrates a "dark" *Betta* cf. *patoti* from East Kalimantan, but its identification is not clear.

Betta cf. *patoti* "EB1" is similar to "Turekai" but with iridescent green scales on the lower body and the gill covers. It also has red below the eye.

Betta cf. *patoti* "Samarinda" is brown with dark vertical bands on the flank and an orange margin on the body at the base of the anal fin. The anal fin has a prominent black submargin and an indistinct white margin. It too has the red mark below the eye. Its fins are heavily spotted. Samarinda is not far from Balikpapan, the type locality of the true *B. patoti*, so this may be the same species. A fish identified as *B. patoti* was collected by Linke from Laut Island off southeast Kalimantan in fast-flowing, rocky-bottomed mountain streams with medium hardness and neutral pH, and even in industrial embayments. The 5 inch

(12.5 cm) fish had a slightly spade-shaped caudal fin and iridescent green scales on the chin and gill covers that did not extend above the level of the eye. (Neither Turekai nor Laut Island is indexed in the *Lonely Planet Guide to Indonesia*.)

Betta sp. "Sangau" is known from Upper Barito River and from Sangau, according to Witte, and is illustrated in Frank Schäfer's *Aqualog* as *Betta* sp. "Sangau." It is reddish brown with rows of iridescent green scales, pointed fins, a spade-shaped caudal, and a thick, dark submargin and a lighter, thin margin in the brown dorsal and anal fins. It is pretty and slender with a large eye and head. Tony Pinto reports it is a mouthbrooder that resembles members of the *B. foerschi* rather than the *B. patoti* group.

Betta unimaculata

B. unimaculata POPTA, 1905 was described from the Howong and Kaja Rivers of Borneo, and has since been found at Barito, Laut Island, Mahakam, and Labuk. It inhabits streams, rivers, ditches, trickles, and puddles, in moderately hard, neutral to slightly basic water (pH 7.5), hidden among vegetation. The populations in the hobby are labeled Kampong Imam and East Tawau. At Bahulak, it occurs in a small, clear water stream over sandstone and above a waterfall in a habitat with no algal growth. Generally it occurs in clear rivers and streams with good flow, but also in clear ponds and irrigation ditches.

B. unimaculata is less than 6 inches (15 cm) long. The males are larger with more intense blue-green with or without iridescence. A broad, blue outer band in the male's anal fin is margined in black on the outside and by black spots on the inside. Horizontal stripes occur in half-grown juveniles and in females.

Some strains of *B. unimaculata* have iridocytes on the gill covers, the entire flanks, or both, and others have a dull (mat) blue color on the body and head. A similar condition in many *B. splendens* is caused by deposits of guanine. In iridescent forms, the guanine is deposited in crystalline layers in the scales, whereas in the mat form the guanine is scattered as particles through the dermis. Guanine crystals in scales are common in *Betta*, and noteworthy in *B. smaragdina* and in the copper form of *B. imbellis*.

Keep a pair in a large covered tank with abundant vegetation and large (3 inch [7.5 cm]) PVC tubes or clay flowerpots as caves. The water should be clear, pH 6.5–7.5, calcium-magnesium hardness 10–20, and temperature 70–77°F (21–25°C). They spawn late in the evening, around 9 or 10 P.M., near the bottom. The female catches the eggs and spits them to the male for brooding. She may remain nearby and guards their territory. The male incubates the 50–80 eggs, and about 10 days later the 0.5 inch (1.3 cm) fry are released and take live *Artemia* nauplii or microworms at once. They grow rapidly even in the parental tank (parents do not eat the fry), reaching half the adult size in 6 months. Maturity takes a year.

Betta ocellata

B. ocellata DE BEAUFORT, 1933 is native to southeastern Sabah in northeastern Borneo. It has been collected from Bettotan, Sandakan, and the Kinbatangan basin, and recently from Tawau by Dennis Yong, who supplied offspring to Tony Pinto in the United States. The adult is brown with a black spot on the caudal peduncle. Males have iridescent blue scales on the gill covers, sometimes a few on the body, but iridescent scales are rare or absent in females. Concentric lines may occur in the dorsal and caudal fins. This fish has been reported incorrectly as a blue form of *Betta unimaculata*.

B. ocellata lives in turbid (muddy) lowland forest streams and river oxbows of the coastal plain, in submerged grasses, leaf litter, and tree roots. According to a Web site of scientists at the National University of Singapore (*www.dbs.nus.edu.sg/research/fish/fightfsh/fightfsh.html*),

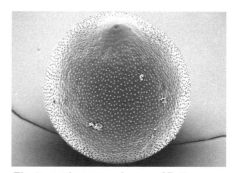

Electron microscope image of Betta ocellata *egg.*

the males pick up the eggs for incubation. This fish has an open-mouth gaping behavior not reported in other species of *Betta*. They are aggressive fish, according to Tony Pinto, and may try to kill each other.

Betta macrostoma

B. macrostoma REGAN, 1909 was described from northern Sarawak and adjacent Brunei, Borneo. It was reported from the Wasah River off the Labi Road and from a waterfall pool in a rain forest near Labi (Brunei), the Sungai River, Sulu National Park, and the upper Mendarem River near Rampayoh. For potential sources of fish, contact the *B. macrostoma* chat club at *bruneibetta@yahoogroups.com*.

The male is orange-brown with a black head dissected by a broad, orange-red band. Black areas below the eye and on the lower half of the gill cover converge at the throat, and are emphasized by black rays in the pectoral fins. The anal fin has a broad, black margin, sometimes with a light edge. The male's dorsal has a thin, white margin and a black spot, not quite an ocellus, at the rear. His caudal fin has a thin, white margin; a

Betta macrostoma, *male.*

broad, black submargin; and two or three broad, black, vertical bands separated by lighter areas. Wild males are far more brilliantly red than domestic stocks in the United States. Out of nuptial coloration, the male has two prominent black horizontal stripes along the flank, a pattern suggesting a partially piscivorous predator.

The female lacks the black face, red central mark, and ocellus. She is lighter with two black horizontal stripes (as in the out-of-nuptial color male), sometimes a peduncular spot, and her caudal fin has only the dark margin. Juveniles have two rows of spots on the body.

This 5 inch (12.5 cm) fish occurs in soft, acidic water (pH 4.3), but does well in neutral water at pH 5.8–7.5, with a soft to moderate calcium-magnesium hardness of 10. It prefers cool temperatures (74–79°F [23–26°C]). Pinter reported the fish from cool, flowing water, and it has been collected at a waterfall.

Feed them fruit flies, brine shrimp, mysid shrimp, bits of fresh edible shrimp, mosquito larvae, frozen adult brine shrimp, frozen bloodworms, and live daphnia. *B. macrostoma* resembles a fierce predator that may also eat guppies. Live foods are best. Overfeeding with frozen foods may cause velvet infections or bacterial disease (dropsy) when leftovers are not promptly siphoned from the bottom. Soft water encourages decomposition, which in turn degrades water quality, making the fish susceptible to velvet and other microbes.

This difficult fish requires highly oxygenated, extremely clean, and soft but nearly neutral water. Mohd Noor Adnin of Brunei recommends at least a 20 gallon (76 L) covered tank, because the fish is a jumper. Ralph Tran uses 30 gallon (114 L) tanks for pairs. Cover the back, sides, and top with black plastic to provide security. Use mostly RO, DI, or rainwater and siphon the bottom regularly to remove uneaten food. Add an outside filter or a large internal sponge filter. Clean the filters and change a third of the tank water every week. The tank should be dense with vegetation and supplied with several 4 inch (10 cm) lengths of 3 inch (7.5 cm) diameter PVC pipe or flowerpot caves. Use an undersized heater that keeps the temperature from falling below 75°F (24°C), because the fish cannot take chilling. This susceptibility to cold also makes it difficult to ship.

If you adhere to these rigorous conditions, you may be rewarded with a spawn. They breed in typical mouthbrooder fashion, the female capturing the eggs and spitting them to the male, who catches and broods them. They usually spawn in the morning over a 4–5 hour period. After breeding, the male's pattern changes to the submissive markings of females with a lighter body and two black horizontal stripes. The eggs hatch in 2 days and the large young (0.25–0.5 inch [0.5–1.0 cm]) are released 3–4 weeks later. The fry stuff themselves with live Artemia nauplii and microworms at once, and reach sexual maturity at 6 months. Males often eat eggs or brooding fry in a community tank or when disturbed. It's advisable to move the male on the third or fourth day to a separate covered, densely vegetated tank of clean water (do not feed him during this time). Richter and Armitage believe that B. macrostoma is allied to the B. unimaculata–B. patoti group.

Populations of Uncertain Status

The status of many stocks is not clear or in flux. Some may be local populations of known species, some will be described and named as valid new species (species nova), some may be useless invalid names applied without a description (nomen nudum), and some may be names applied to fishes solely on the basis of photographs with no locality or other useful information (species inquirenda), so we don't know if they are valid or not.

Betta sp. "Bangka."

Betta *sp. "Bung Bihn."*

Betta *sp. "Mandor."*

Betta cf. *akarensis, Betta* sp. Sanggau, *Betta* sp. Antonii, and Porca Betta are all the same fish. Sanggau is in East Kalimantan.

Betta sp. "Bangka"—Bangka is an island off Sumatra. Pinto believes this is a mouthbrooder in the *pugnax* group.

Betta sp. "Bung Bihn."

Betta sp. (*schalleri*) sp. E.

Betta sp. (*schalleri*) sp. F.

Betta sp. "Jantur Gemeruh."

Betta sp. "Kapuas"—possibly *B. dimidiata*. The Kapuas River drains West Kalimantan.

Betta sp. "Sukadana" is a brilliant red member of the *coccina* group from western Kalimantan, Borneo.

Betta schalleri.

Betta sp. "Medes," "Medas," or "Golden Sphinx"—a *waseri* type fish with deep red eyes.

Betta sp. "Sanpit"—not to be confused with Sapit, east of the Sunda Shelf.

Betta sp. "Sintang"—city in the middle of West Kalimantan on the Kapuas River.

Betta cf. *strohi, Betta* sp. "Mandor"—Mandor is in southwestern Kalimantan.

Betta sp. "Tayan."

Betta sp. "Southern Thailand"—Southern Thailand is just north of the Malay Peninsula. The fish called *Betta* sp. "Southern Thailand" resembles *B. prima* but was reportedly being described as a new species by Maurice Kottelat. One (unreliable) difference is that *B. prima* has a rounded caudal fin, and "Southern Thailand" has a spade-shaped caudal fin. The fish was spawned by Nonn Panitvong, who reported that it is a typical mouthbrooder. Pinto, who has firsthand knowledge of this fish, believes it is *B. prima*, and has previously had bettas with round tails develop spade-shaped tails with age.

Chapter Five

Foods and Feeding

In nature, wild fish never have nutritional deficiencies. In a home aquarium, aquarists often put convenience ahead of needs. How healthy would you be if you ate nothing but bread? Now imagine what an insectivorous betta thinks of canned flake food! If you want robust, healthy adult bettas, and fast-growing, healthy fry, give them the kind of nutrition you don't find in a can of dried food.

Wild bettas eat mites, spiders, flies, mosquitoes, daphnia, ostracods, amphipods, snails, aquatic worms, and an occasional small fish. Worms and insects are rich in proteins and lipids (fats and oils). Bettas get the useless carbohydrate chitin from insect and crustacean shells, the useful carbohydrate glycogen from insect and worm muscle, and minerals from everything, including snails and clams. Flake foods are primarily cereal grains that will make a fish fat but not healthy.

Bettas use simple molecules from digestion to make complex molecules for growth and health. However, bettas cannot make every kind of substance; some substances have to be provided in the diet. These "essential" substances include some amino acids and several unsaturated fatty acids. There are no essential carbohydrates. Other required substances are the water-soluble vitamins in yeast, the fat-soluble vitamins in oils, and highly unsaturated fatty acids, explained below.

Lipids (fats, fatty acids, oils) are used for energy, sex hormones, cell membranes, and the brain and nervous system. The most important are the essential long-chain HUFAs. If they are not in the diet, baby fish die or fail to grow, and older fish age prematurely or develop abnormalities. Brine shrimp nauplii are rich in HUFAs at hatching, but lose them after 24 hours. Other rich HUFA sources are insects, crustaceans, fish liver oil, annelid worms, and egg yolk.

The most nutritional foods for adult bettas are insects—mosquito larvae, fruit flies (*Drosophila*), glass worms (*Chaoborus*), bloodworms or midges (chironomids), and baby crickets (for large bettas). Glass worms are the larvae of winter flies, which are seasonally available at pet stores or can be collected in winter from under the ice of frozen ponds.

Artemia and *Daphnia* are crustaceans and are not very nutritious. More nutritious crustaceans are the copepods, mysids, and euphausids. Other rich foods are the annelid worms, such as chopped earthworms, and live black worms, tubifex, microfex, white worms, and grindal worms. Also important, mostly to fry, are the nematode worms called microworms and vinegar eels.

Adult fish are easy to keep because they are fully formed. Baby fish are more difficult because we have fewer foods for a complete diet, they are crowded, and they are under more stress. It's easy to keep a hundred grown fish, but a hundred fry is a challenge to raise.

The principal aquarium foods for baby fishes are (a) the newly hatched eggs (cysts) of brine shrimp we call brine shrimp nauplii, (b) small nematodes we call microworms and vinegar eels, and (c) the mixture of protozoans, rotifers, gastrotrichs, and other microscopic animals we call infusoria.

Foods for Fry

Protozoa and Rotifers

In nature, the first food of bubblenester fry are the protozoa, rotifers, and other microbes that glide over submerged vegetation or swim within colonies of single-celled algae. (The fry of mouthbrooders are larger and do not require such tiny foods.) In Asia, commercial breeders put dried tree leaves in the breeding containers to provide a floating support for the bubblenest, and to decay as a food source for protozoans.

Protozoans are easy to culture. An inoculum (starter culture) of *Paramecium* or of *Coleps* can be ordered through aquarium magazines, scientific supply houses, or the Internet (*www.aquaculturestore.com*). *Paramecium* eat mostly bacteria and floating algal cells. Put the starter culture into a gallon of aged tap water, and drop in a single dried split pea half. Adding another dried split pea half once a week should maintain the culture. You will see the protozoans as fine white spots in the water. Overfeeding will cause a bacterial bloom, a murky film, as the culture is overgrown with bacteria that kill the protozoans. Always keep backup cultures for this contingency. If bacteria overwhelm the protozoans, you must start over. Another good food you can buy and culture is the freshwater rotifer *Brachionus*. Rotifers are larger than many protozoa, but more difficult to culture. Rotifers are raised on green water (algae cultures) or special commercial foods.

You don't need a pure culture or *Paramecium* or *Brachionus*. You can make an infusoria culture of mixed *Paramecium* and *Coleps*. Place a dried leaf from a hardwood tree (such as oak, maple, or sycamore), some dried grass, a banana skin, or a lettuce leaf in a jar of water from your aquarium or use stagnant water from an outdoor pool, pond, ditch, or container. After a week on a window sill, protozoans in the water will have grazed over the surface of the leaf (banana, lettuce, and so on) and multiplied into thousands. Hold the jar up to the light. Noxious bacterial blooms are solid gray and the water has a foul odor; throw this away. Successful protozoan blooms have no unpleasant odor, and clouds resolve as fine white dustlike specks of ciliates. If there are no clouds and the water remains clear, all the protozoans are attached to the dead vegetation, and these are probably *Coleps,* a larger, stiffer ciliate that scavenges dead vegetation. Both *Coleps* and *Paramecium* are excellent first foods for small fry. If you have a microscope, swirl the jar and observe a drop of water under the lens. *Paramecium* swim in all directions. *Coleps* are larger and attached. Bacteria are invisible or appear as vibrating specks.

To use a culture, swirl the jar vigorously to distribute the protozoans, suck up the culture water with a food baster, and squirt the contents into the fry tank. Keep multiple cultures, because they eventually become polluted with bacteria, fail, and must be replaced.

Liquid Fry Foods

You can find liquid fry foods in squeeze tubes at your local pet store. I don't use them because they can spoil from heat or age, or become contaminated with yeast or bacteria. They are as likely to cause the growth of bacteria as of the fry, and are too risky in my opinion.

Dry Fry Foods

A commercial aquaculture product, Larva "Z" diet (Zeigler Brothers, Gardners, Pennsylvania, *www.zeiglerfeed.com*), has a high content of cholesterol, phospholipids, xanthophylls, and 5 percent by weight of HUFAs. It is sold as a substitute for live *Artemia* nauplii, and comes in fine grades that substitute for infusoria. The feeds are packaged in semibuoyant microparticles of less than 100 through more than 450 microns in 50 micron intervals. (A micron is equal to 1/1,000th of a millimeter, and there are 25.4 mm in an inch.) Chemical attractants are included in the formulation.

Algae

Many green and some blue-green algae (*Spirulina*) contain HUFAs, carotenoids, oils, and other essential substances. They are used to feed and enrich protozoan, rotifer, and *Daphnia* cultures. Because algae are often contaminated with protozoans that graze on them, green water cultures from outdoors are usually a good first food for baby bubblenesters.

Nematodes

Microworms and vinegar eels are minute roundworms (nematodes). Both are rich foods for fry less than a week old, and a valuable supplement bridging the period between infusoria and *Artemia* nauplii. Both grow on yeast and bacteria, and are grown from starter cultures that you can order from magazines or the Internet (*www.jehmco.com*).

For vinegar eels, buy some apple cider vinegar. Dilute it by half with tap water. Add a slice of apple, cover, pour in starter culture, and wait. In 2 weeks you will have a thriving culture, visible as a white line under the surface. To make a new culture, take a portion and inoculate it into another jar of apple cider vinegar and water. To use the culture, swirl the jar and pour off a portion, or remove the white ring with a food baster, then filter it through a gold coffee filter or brine shrimp nauplii net. Invert the net or filter into a container of tap water, and baste or pour the concentrated worms into the tank with the baby fish.

For microworms, clean some plastic butter or margarine tubs and their lids. Make a paste of mixed flaked baby food with water, and place a layer on the bottom of a plastic tub. Add a sprinkle of baker's yeast granules and mix it into the paste. Place a smear of old (or starter) microworm culture to the paste and replace the cover. Slit the cover to allow carbon dioxide gas to escape from the growing yeast. After a few days, the yeast has multiplied, and the microworms now swarm over the surface eating the yeast. Many of them climb the walls of the tub. Use your finger to wipe the worms from the walls. Swirl your finger in water to release them, and then baste or pour the worms to your baby fish. In 2 to 3 weeks the culture becomes overripe with too much yeast, foul smelling, blackened, and liquefied, and the worms no longer climb the walls. Begin a new culture (or two) and discard this one, using it only for starter material. The new culture does not need yeast, because you will transfer enough with the inoculum of worms.

Brine Shrimp (*Artemia*)

The best fry food are newly hatched brine shrimp (nauplii). Small packets of brine shrimp eggs (cysts) are seldom air-tight, take up humidity, and produce the poorest hatches. The best hatches are from vacuum-packed 15 ounce (425 g) cans seldom seen in pet stores, but sold by companies such as Aquatic Eco-Systems and Argent, mail-order companies (*www.brineshrimpdirect.com* or *www.jehmco.com*), or other Internet sources. Just search *www.google.com* for "brine shrimp." The higher the hatch rate, the higher the price. Open the can with a punch can opener, pour a portion into a screw-top jar for 2 weeks of hatchings, cover the can with a tight-fitting plastic lid, and store the can in a freezer until you need to refill your jar. Water vapor in air kills eggs and reduces the hatch, whereas storage in a freezer prolongs useful life by pulling water vapor out of the air.

The hatchlings are called nauplii, and are smallest and rich in HUFAs for the first 24 hours. By then, the nutritive value has dropped off as they use up their fatty acids, and the nauplii double in size.

Hatch the cysts in a gallon jar of synthetic sea water with strong aeration under strong light. After 36 hours, remove the air, swirl the contents, and pour the slurry through a brine shrimp net (an aquarium net lined with a cloth similar to that of a handkerchief). After straining, invert the net with the eggshells and nauplii into a larger jar of cold tap water. After 10 minutes, the nauplii have sunk to the bottom and the empty shells float at the surface. Pour off the water and floating shells, and then wipe the remaining shells from the walls with your finger and throw them away. Top off the jar with new tap water, swirl, and feed the cleaned nauplii (without the shells) to your fish with a food baster. Nauplii are the best food for fry after the infusoria stage, and can even be the staple for adult fish.

Foods for Larger Bettas

Crustaceans
Brine Shrimp

Brine shrimp (*Artemia*) are salt-loving cousins of the freshwater fairy shrimp genus *Stephanolepis*. They are crustaceans (Branchiopoda: Anostraca) that occur around the world in temporary, ephemeral, and vernal (seasonal) fish-free pools and ponds. The most common brine shrimp sold in the United States is *Artemia franciscana* from California and Utah and other places around

Large can of brine shrimp eggs.

the world. Another species, *A. monica*, occurs in Mono Lake, California, but is not in commercial supply. Others include *A. tunisiana, A. urminiana,* and *A. salina*. The adults of *Artemia franciscana* are collected by net from salt-drying ponds in California, but the bulk of the American supply is cultured in greenhouses and sold by a Florida company.

Brine shrimp reproduce sexually and parthenogenetically. The dark brown eggs (cysts) are gathered from windrows on the shores of salt lakes. The aquarium hobby gets less than 5 percent of the harvest, the remainder going to the aquaculture industry for farming food shrimp and fish. Most bettas take newly hatched brine as a first food and throughout life.

To grow your own adult brine shrimp, fill a large container with old sea water or brine shrimp hatch water, add vigorous aeration and

Hatching brine shrimp eggs.

ponds. Fairy shrimp are sometimes available from the classified section of aquarium magazines or scientific supply houses. Fairy shrimp produce eggs that hatch quickly and cysts that provide next season's population (resting eggs).

In the eastern United States we have *Eubranchipus* and *Stephano-lepis.* In California, *Branchinecta conservio* is federally protected, so don't harvest fairy shrimp on the West Coast. They all grow to more than one inch in outdoor pools with green water or sprinkled with *Spirulina* powder as food. Adults are colorless, green, or red, and must be continually harvested to keep them from eating young produced by summer eggs. The adults are eaten by the larger mouthbrooders and the juveniles are appropriate for all bettas. The life cycle is short. The bottom of the container should be siphoned weekly, filtered, and used to inoculate other cultures immediately (summer eggs) or dried on newspaper. The dried paper with its detritus and eggs is packed in envelopes in the refrigerator for hatching at a future date.

Opossum Shrimp

Opossum shrimp are nutritious crustaceans of the family Mysidae. They average 70 percent protein, 8 percent fats and oils, 2–3 percent fiber, and 5–6 percent ash. Their oils are dominated by the two most important HUFAs, known as EPA (eicosapentaenoic acid) and DHA (dodecahexaenoic acid) and caro-

intense overhead light, and inoculate the water with a small amount of hatched nauplii (not eggs). Feed lightly with a liquefied suspension of baker's yeast in water once a week; dry yeast will sink and cause bacterial blooms. Unicellular algae (green water) are better and are consumed rapidly.

Fairy Shrimp

Fairy shrimp occur worldwide in fish-free freshwater lakes and tenoids. Opossum shrimp females carry their young in a brood pouch. You can grow them in 10 gallon (38 L) tanks, pools, or barrels. They eat *Artemia* nauplii and their own young, so adults are screened off to provide a refugium where babies can escape and grow up. Adults can be in a screen-bottomed container, or the tank can be divided with a screen.

Most mysids are salt-loving creatures, but a few live in freshwater. *Mysis relicta* lives in deep lakes of the Northern Hemisphere where it is one of the kinds of plankton that provide food for trout and salmon fry. When introduced into Canada's Lake Ookenagen to enhance the fishery for kokanee salmon, it came to dominate the lake without providing any kokanee salmon benefits because the mysids migrated down to the bottom during the day when the baby fish migrated to the surface, and vice versa. Piscine Energetics is the main source of frozen mysids in the hobby, all harvested from this lake. They also ship live mysids that must be kept in the refrigerator where they can survive a week or more. Adult mysids are 0.75 inch (2 cm), but you can order juveniles. Most bettas take the juvenile grade, and larger mouth-brooders take adult mysids. For live or frozen freshwater mysids, contact Piscine Energetics, 32 Baxter Road, Enderby, BC, VOE 1VO, Canada, *granberg@mail.junction.net*. For estuarine and marine mysids, contact Bio-Marine Aquafauna at P.O. Box 5, Hawthorne, CA 90250, *aquafauna@aquafauna.com*. For a live starter cul-

Mysids (opossum shrimp).

ture of mysids, search *www.google.com* or the yellow pages under "Laboratories, Testing."

Water Fleas

Daphnia, Ceriodaphnia, and related cladocerans are called water fleas. They are crustaceans and not fleas (insects). Frozen daphnia are available in pet stores or from *www.brineshrimpdirect.com*.

Wild live *Daphnia pulex* or the much larger *Daphnia magna* may be purchased from some pet stores but are seasonal, and the supply is unreliable. *Ceriodaphnia* is used by bioassay laboratories because of its smaller size and faster reproduction. Look for it in your telephone book under "Laboratories, Testing." See the advertisements in aquarium magazines for starter cultures.

Daphnia can be raised outdoors in daylight during the summer. Fill a barrel or pool with tap water, and throw in some dirt. The dirt stimulates an algal bloom. When the water

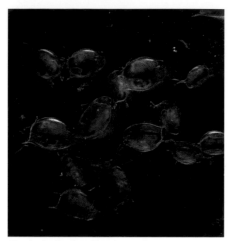
Daphnia *(water fleas).*

becomes green, add starter *Daphnia*. When the *Daphnia* become abundant, harvest them with a coarse net so the young escape to replenish the population. With time, production drops and the water yellows. Change some of the water to dilute wastes and add garden soil to replenish nutrients. Keeping several outdoor cultures is better, because most cultures eventually crash, and you don't want to be left without one. Winter weather depresses production but doesn't kill the culture. The *Daphnia* eggs will survive winter and the population will bloom again in spring. On the other hand, full sun and summer temperatures can kill a culture by removing oxygen from the water.

You can grow *Daphnia* indoors in 10 gallon (38 L) tanks, but any wide and shallow container with large surface area works. Place a bright light (I prefer a shop light with two 40 W, 4 foot [1 m] bulbs) directly over a

tank on the floor (to keep it cool) lined on the sides and bottom with aluminum foil. Fill with tap water, dechlorinate, and provide strong aeration with stiff tubing (to produce large bubbles) but not an air stone, because fine bubbles mist and can short-circuit your light fixture. Fertilize with liquid plant food, and inoculate with green water to start the tank toward becoming green with algae. It will take a few weeks to get the *Daphnia* population large enough for daily harvest. Feed the *Daphnia* additional green water or a slurry of (never granular) baker's yeast. Pour a tablespoonful of dry yeast into 1 gallon (4 L) of tap water, and leave it at room temperature for 2 days, by which time the yeast will have grown rapidly and fouled the water. Then store the jar of yeast culture in the refrigerator to keep it from growing further. Every 2 days, pour a small amount of yeast culture into the *Daphnia* tank. Overfeeding kills the cladocerans, whereas underfeeding only slows their growth. Periodically siphon most of the water and sediments from the bottom, and replace with new tap water, because the accumulation of waste products slows production. Eventually, the culture fails from its pollutant load that eliminates oxygen and must be restarted by draining and cleaning the tank with hot water and beginning anew. Don't use brewer's yeast, which is dead and will not provide a growing food for the *Daphnia*. Watch for infestations with *Hydra* that will wipe out the baby cladocerans. You can eliminate *Hydra* with Panacur (see the chapter on diseases). *Daphnia* should be cultured between 60° and 70°F (16° and 21°C).

Moina

Moina is a dwarf cladoceran smaller than *Ceriodaphnia*, and cultured like *Daphnia,* except that it does better than *Daphnia* in warm water (over 70°F [21°C]). It is suitable to indoor culture in gallon jars, small tanks, or shoe boxes. *Moina* are so small as to require a magnifying glass, but their multiplication rate and culture density exceed that of *Daphnia*. They are excellent for small bettas. Some species of *Moina* live in brine ponds and alkaline soda (salt) lakes from the American West to Australia, but are not yet cultured for the aquarium hobby.

Scuds

Scuds (*Hyalella*) are small (less than 0.25 inch [0.6 cm]) bottom-dwelling amphipods (Crustacea) that scavenge decayed food, detritus, and dead animals. A nutritious food for bettas, they help maintain water quality through consumption of waste that otherwise would feed bacteria. *Gammarus* are a slightly larger kind of scud. All scuds can be cultured in a fish-free tank with plants to absorb nitrogenous wastes and dried hardwood leaves as food, supplemented with frozen foods (such as brine shrimp). Harvest by swirling a net to pick up detritus, empty the contents into a wide-mouth container of water,

and swirl the water and decant until the detritus is removed and the scuds are concentrated. You cannot over-feed your fish with scuds. Any survivors will hide and eventually be consumed.

Copepods

Copepods are the most nutritious, abundant, and ubiquitous food source in nature for almost all larval fishes. They are the most important part of the zooplankton. Culture of copepods is difficult, and especially of appropriate copepods that will be eaten by the fish, instead of vice versa. See *www.aims.gov.au/pages/ research/hatchery-feeds/pdf/cope pod-culture-manual.pdf* for guidance.

One newly available copepod that grows almost as a monoculture in a saline lake (pH 9.7, salinity 72 ppt) in northern Canada is marketed as CYCLOP-EEZE. The product is a source of the carotenoid pigment astaxanthin and the HUFAs, EPA, and DCA. Upon harvest, the copepods are deep frozen aboard ship, and blocks are then taken to the Argent Company plant for freeze-drying (lyophilization).

Cyclop-eeze is rich in fatty acids (35 percent), especially the HUFAs EPA (11.74 percent) and DHA (11.09 percent). Some 94 percent of carotenoids of Cyclop-eeze is astaxanthin. Test feed reports showed that dietary astaxanthin esters result in pigmentation several times higher than either chemical astaxanthin or other pigment sources. Growth enhancement is 15–30 percent, and

Parameters	Cyclop-eeze	Artemia
Protein	60%	73%
Lipid	35	18
Ash	3	5
Carbohydrate	2	3
Astaxanthin	3000 ppm	<D.L.
Canthaxanthin	15 ppm	102 ppm
18:3n3 (Linolenic Acid)	10.45%	1.3%
20:5n3 (EPA)	11.74%	0.25%
22:6n3 (DHA)	11.09%	2.7%
Enzyme Activity		
(Superoxide Dismutase)	30,000	22,500
Average Body Length	800 µm	400 µm

reproductive enhancement is 5–15 percent. If your local pet dealer does not have this product, you can order Cyclop-eeze through mail order suppliers, such as Jehmco, or aquaculture suppliers, such as Argent or Aquatic Eco-Systems.

Oligochaetes
Earthworms

The best-known oligochaetes are terrestrial earthworms. Small earthworms (red wigglers) can be purchased at fishing bait outlets or cultured in boxes of worm bedding and peat moss and fed moistened bread. A simple way to accumulate earthworms is by maintaining a large pile of dead leaves outdoors on pavement. Worms will collect at the bottom. Another method for collecting them is pouring salt water on the ground. The worms will come out within minutes. Chopped earthworms are highly nutritious and a good food for larger mouthbrooders.

White Worms and Grindal Worms

White worms and grindal worms are terrestrial oligochaetes related to earthworms. Starter cultures are available through classified advertisements. Both are rich in fats and proteins, and when vitamins or other nutrients are added to their food, they ingest them and become carriers of these additional nutrients. Statements that these foods are "starchy" are incorrect; starches occur only in plants. Statements that these foods can cause fatty degeneration are also unsupported. Both white worms and grindal worms are exceptionally nutritious, and many breeders use them to condition adults for spawning. The two species differ in size and temperature tolerance (grindal worms can be stored at room temperature and are smaller, whereas the larger white worms must be kept cold). Start a covered wooden or Styrofoam box with earthworm bedding soil or a mixture of peat moss and potting soil. Add barely enough water to slightly darken the mix. Add starter culture and a slice of white bread or a heaping tablespoonful of flaked baby food or cornmeal on the surface or into a slit in the surface, plus just enough milk or water to moisten the food. Cover the food site with a glass pane, and store the culture at high refrigerator temperatures (white worms) or cool basement temperatures (grindal worms). If the culture dries out, the worms will be killed. Periodically, lift the glass pane to harvest the worms, and feed them to adult fish. Replace bread, flakes, or cornmeal as necessary, and monitor moisture. Eventually, the culture will be contaminated with black sewage flies (midges), which are annoying but do no harm. If you can harvest the flies, feed them to your fighting fish. Always maintain multiple cultures as backups.

Black Worms, Tubifex, and Microfex

Black worms and tubifex worms are freshwater aquatic oligochaetes of the family Tubificidae. Both consist of a mix of species in the family Tubificidae. You can purchase portions at pet stores, and some stores will make special orders if you buy a few pounds at a time. Red tubifex are abundant in wastewater and years ago were collected below sewage treatment plants. With changes in treatment mandated by the Clean Water Act, the large mats of red tubifex of years past are not seen in the United States today, but

can still be bought in Mexico, the source of most red tubifex today. Red tubifex tolerate warm water and low levels of chlorine. Keep them in a jar in a sink under slowly running cold water. The water washes out their stomach contents and any dead worms. The purged worms are highly nutritious. Black worms are large coldwater tubificids that collect on the screens of trout farm raceways and in the effluent treatment ponds of vegetable processors in California. Black worms are intolerant of heat, chlorine, and pollution, and cannot be maintained with running tap water, but should be stored in shallow dishes in the refrigerator. Daily, they should be swirled with cold, dechlorinated tap water, and the washings discarded. Keep 1 gallon (4 L) of tap water in the refrigerator to maintain a supply of dechlorinated cold water. Black worms die quickly in their own pollutants, and cannot be stored more than a few weeks. Both black worms and red tubifex will establish and even reproduce in the gravel in community tanks, but not in jars. They can be cultivated much like microfex worms. Bettas may engorge on black worms, resulting in gastric distress and sometimes death. Many aquarists cut them into pieces with a razor blade before feeding them to bettas. Black worms that survive partial ingestion can tear the stomachs of small fish, killing them. Both black worms and red tubifex worms may carry pathogenic bacteria, and should be purged before feeding to bettas. They some-

A nutritious diet is crucial to your betta's good health.

times transmit parasitic worms infectious for suckers and catfish, but not bettas.

Microfex worms are much smaller aquatic oligochaetes of the family Naididae, which differ from Tubificidae by size and by an odd proboscis that may be as long as the worm. The only important genus is *Dero*. Kent Webster, who got his start from Jim Langhammer, offers mixed cultures of *Dero* worms and *Daphnia magna* on e-Bay. Webster and Langhammer advise setting up multiple tanks on the floor, using heavy feeding (daily or every other day) with *Spirulina* flakes, some yeast, cool water with strong aeration and frequent water changes. Webster's cultures come with *Daphnia magna* but Langhammer also keeps Gammarus

in the same tanks. Culture tanks need continuous light to support the *Daphnia,* and massive daily water changes to enable heaviest feeding. Langhammer changes 75 percent a day. Both Langhammer and Webster feed daily, but advise beginners to not feed again until the water clears. With insufficient feeding, the culture dies off; with heavy feeding it doubles and triples in short order. Without water changes, the culture crashes. Webster coined the term "microfex" to describe what resemble minute red tubifex, although these worms are in a different family.

Insects
Bloodworms and Midges

Bloodworms are the larvae of the insect family Chironomidae, commonly called sewage flies or midges. They are the principal food of most freshwater fishes around the world. The commercial supply is harvested from Asian duck farm ponds for the aquarium market. They cost more than frozen brine shrimp, are more nutritious, and are rich in proteins and oils, including HUFAs. Thaw the block before feeding your fish. Frozen chunks of food can damage a fish's stomach and cause death.

You can grow bloodworms outdoors. Fill a wading pool or barrel with water, and add twigs and dead leaves. Within weeks all the surfaces will have thousands of thin, brown capsules 0.5 inch (1.3 cm) long containing individual bloodworms. Scrape them off and shake to release the bloodworms. Our native bloodworms are smaller than the Asian product. You can wash these first or feed them to your fish, mud and all. Live bloodworms are now shipped from Asia into the United States in small breathable Kordon packages that keep the animals alive for up to 2 weeks. The bags are pervious to carbon dioxide and oxygen, but not to water.

Some people are allergic to bloodworms. The allergy is linked to certain bloodworm proteins. If you get flulike symptoms when handling bloodworms, stop using them and consult a physician. The initial reaction is usually mild, but subsequent exposures often cause increasingly severe reactions.

Fruit Flies

Vestigial winged (nonflying) fruit flies (*Drosophila*) can be grown in narrow-neck jars plugged with cotton or foam so air is freely exchanged while flies are retained inside. The flies feed on yeast that grows on a paste of culture medium that can be flaked baby food or mashed potato flakes enriched with corn (Karo) syrup and a mold inhibitor. The small white maggots pupate on the glass walls and paper in the jars. When the flies hatch, the jar is tamped to make them fall, then inverted and the top removed to shake them out and quickly replugged. The harvested flies are sprinkled on top of the water and greedily consumed by all anabantoids. Order starter cultures from ads in aquarium magazines or Carolina Biological Supply in Burlington, NC (*carolina@carolina.com*). This nutritious food is some trouble, because you need many cultures for daily feedings and must continually make new cultures. It is worth the effort, especially for wild bettas that may not readily take to frozen foods. Powdered vitamins and paprika shaken in a plastic bag with fruit flies will stick to the flies, enhancing their nutritive value.

Prepared Foods

Flakes and Granules

Most beginners buy expensive flake foods, often selecting a package with a pretty picture or the word "betta" in the label. Many commercial breeders use generic flake food for grow-out because it is cheap, and easy to handle and store. If you want to use a flake food, pick one that is meat based, with minimal plant matter. Read the order of the ingredients. If the first items listed are grains, the food is unsuitable. Always select foods with first ingredients of shrimp, fish, or insects. I recommend commercial trout chow granules for bettas. Trout are insectivores, and their chows have been formulated for aquaculture to meet this requirement. Bettas are also largely insectivores, so no prepared food is better. A test of commercial trout chow versus a popular brand of aquarium flake food at the University of Hawaii confirmed trout chow's nutritional superiority.

Some dry foods are of high quality. Those with *Spirulina* (blue-green algae) are rich in the carotenoid astaxanthin and are color enhancing. Mike Reed's foods are popular with breeders for their egg yolk, other additives, and attractants (Mike Reed Enterprises, P.O. Box 1930, Sutter Creek, CA 95685, *www.mreed.com*). Betta Bio-Gold from Hikari is primarily shrimp meal, fish meal, yeast, and vitamins. Betta-Min from Tetra is mostly fish meal, with rice as an extender, supplemented with yeast, shrimp meal, algae meal, fish oil (a HUFA source), lecithin, and vitamin C. If you use dried foods, mix or alternate several to increase variety in the diet.

Freeze-dried Foods

Freeze-dried krill (Euphausiid shrimp, major marine zooplankters) are rich in proteins and oils, including HUFAs and carotenoids. The krill dust in the package is a useful fry food. Other freeze-dried foods have less nutritive value, and some, such as tubificid worms, may spread disease because they may not be purged of sewage bacteria before dehydrating.

Paste Foods

Most breeders make their own paste foods, an idea proposed by Dr. Myron Gordon and loosely called Gordon's formula. The basic paste is a meat as the main ingredient (beef heart or fish fillet) supplemented with raw egg, raw shrimp, fresh spinach, raw liver, a multivitamin, cod liver oil, lecithin (from a drugstore), color enhancer (*Spirulina* powder), and a gelatin binder. Variations include adding squid entrails, fish roe, insects, dried krill, and other sources of HUFAs. The meat is picked to remove tough fibers that can lodge in the throat or gut, and blended until smooth with the other ingredients and enough water to make a paste consistency. The paste is (usually) heated with gelatin, but some people prefer to use entirely raw paste, and others don't use the gelatin binder. In the last step, the paste is spooned into plastic bags and laid flat in a freezer. As needed, a bag is opened and a piece of frozen paste broken off, thawed, and fed to the fish.

Chapter Six

Common Diseases and Treatments

Bettas can become sick from intolerable temperatures, chemicals, or diseases. We may not recognize the condition until it is too late to save the fish. It's important to watch your fish carefully, especially after a water change with tap water, the introduction of new fishes to their aquarium, discovery of a faulty heater, a power outage that causes a temperature drop, overfeeding, or feeding with a live food from an outdoor source.

Physical and Chemical Effects

Temperature

Fighting fish in the wild occur at a temperature range of 70–90°F (21–32°C). However, your fish may be intolerant of this wide range. Every fish adapts to upper and lower temperatures during the early larval stage, a capability it loses as it grows older. If young fry are held at a narrow temperature, they will be unable to survive widely fluctuating temperatures later in life. If they are exposed to widely fluctuating temperatures in the first days, they develop tolerance for wide temperature ranges into adulthood. For this reason, pond-raised fish are typically more temperature tolerant than those raised in heated indoor hatcheries. If you want your fry to have a wide temperature tolerance, grow them without heaters and allow normal room temperature fluctuations in their tanks.

High temperatures reduce the dissolved oxygen concentration in water. Low oxygen levels of 2 or 3 parts per million (ppm) are stressful, and below 2 ppm can be lethal. Normal oxygen levels should be 5–7 or more ppm. Under low-oxygen (hypoxic) conditions, bettas rise to the surface to gulp air into the labyrinth for supplemental oxygen. Low oxygen conditions in nature are usually caused by decaying vegetation, not heated water. The labyrinth is not effective when heat drives the oxygen out of the water. Heat can cause irreversible tissue damage.

Cold temperatures may make the fish lethargic. Prolonged, deep cold

Flexibacter *infection.*

depresses the immune system, so ordinarily harmless microbes become invasive and pathogenic. Aquarium thermostats on heaters corrode with age and stick, so the heater never turns off. More aquarium fish die as a result of faulty heaters than of cold. Serious breeders heat the room rather than the tanks. It's safer, cheaper, and easier. Heaters fail and cook fish, or they may break and provide an electric shock when you work in that tank.

If you live in the far north in a cold house, you may need a heater or you may want one for inducing breeding. Manufacturers recommend 5 watts per gallon, so a 10 gallon (38 L) tank should get a 50-watt heater and a 20 gallon (76 L) tank a 100-watt heater. If the thermostat fails, the heating element runs continuously and the tank can reach 100°F (38°C) or more. At such a high temperature, dissolved oxygen in the water approaches zero, and the labyrinth is of no use because the gill membranes and respiratory enzymes are irreversibly

damaged. Fish exposed to these temperatures might be rescued, but will shortly die.

That's why I recommend undersizing your heater. With a damaged thermostat, the smaller unit will be incapable of overheating the tank or, at worst, overheat it more slowly, giving you time to correct the condition. An undersized heater will not quickly or efficiently restore the correct temperature, and it may not raise it where you would prefer, but it will still mitigate occasional chilling.

The heater least likely to fail is one with an electronic thermostat. These heaters cost more, but seldom overheat. An alternative is to use cheap heaters and replace them annually so they don't accumulate enough corrosion on the contacts to cause sticking and overheating.

Chlorine

Chlorine is the most common killer of aquarium fishes. Chlorinated tap water can kill fishes within minutes. Simply allowing tap water to stand and evaporate chlorine is unreliable, because some tap water will not lose enough to be safe even in 48 hours, and the use of chloramines by some municipalities renders evaporation useless. Municipal utilities usually add ammonia to chlorine during the warm months to convert unstable chlorine to stable chloramines that last longer in the distribution system. Chloramine is stable even at 175°F (79°C) for up to 3 days. Commercial dechlorinators and dechloraminators that include sodium thiosulfate and ammonia removers remove both chlorine and chloramines.

pH

Many communities use water from high pH limestone aquifers. Others have high manganese levels, or fungal or blue-green algae in their reservoirs that produce noxious colors, tastes, or odors. Sometimes the treatment (as with potassium hydroxide) creates tap water with an unusually high pH. The Siamese fighting fish comes from lowland swamps with low pH values, and other species from hillside streams may be adapted to *slightly* basic pH values up to 7.8. But tap water with a pH of 10 is common in some communities, and this level is unsafe. High pH may strain the fish's ability to maintain osmotic balance in the surrounding water, because pH affects its ability to osmoregulate calcium and potassium ions across the gill membranes. More important, a high pH dangerously shifts the equilibrium between ammonia (NH_3) and ammonium (NH_4) ions. Ammonia is toxic, but ammonium is nontoxic. At low or acidic pH values (6–4), the equilibrium shifts toward ammonium ions, and most waste ammonia from metabolism is rendered harmless. At high pH values, the equilibrium shifts the other way, with toxic ammonia dominating the equilibrium. The same waste product that is toxic at high pH is nontoxic at low pH.

The ammonia-ammonium equilibrium is important when shipping bettas. Until a few years ago, shippers added pH buffer to the shipping bag water to maintain neutral pH during transit. When shippers did not add buffer, the survival rate was better, even when the water was of extremely the low pH. This demonstrated that ammonia, not pH, is the important concern when shipping fish.

Air

During winter, tap water is colder and absorbs more gasses from the atmosphere. When that water warms, the increased temperature lets the water release the supersaturated gases. If you fill a tank with dechlorinated tap water in winter, bubbles often appear on the glass. Those bubbles can also attach to gills, causing oxidation or irreversible burning of the tissues. When you set up a tank with new water, give it a full day or two for the temperature and gases to equilibrate before adding fish.

Carbon Dioxide

Carbon dioxide is a waste gas of metabolism. Its normal concentration in water is almost undetectable, and even in air it amounts to perhaps 1 percent. If fish are shipped in an ordinary plastic bag and no air space is available for venting carbon dioxide, the fish will become anaesthetized by the gas and then stop breathing and die. When shipping bettas in ordinary plastic bags, use one-third water and two-thirds of the bag volume for air. The large space provides

Unpacking Shipped Fish

Fish received by mail should be unpacked in darkness or dim light. Regular fish bags should be floated in the aquarium for temperature equilibration at least an hour. Afterward, the water should be gradually poured out and discarded (not placed in the tank), and replaced with tank water over a period of perhaps 30 minutes. At the end of this period, the contents of the bag should be poured through a net, the water discarded, and the fish lowered into the receiving tank. The net should then be sterilized with hot tap water and dried. This prevents potential pathogens in shipping water from getting into your tank. Keep the new fish in dim light for 24 hours, and treat the water with Melafix according to directions (overdoses can be lethal). Melafix assists in slime formation and protects wounds from becoming infected. If possible, new fish should be quarantined for at least a week before being mixed with other fishes.

a reservoir of oxygen (air is 21 percent oxygen) and space for venting carbon dioxide that diffuses from the higher concentration in water to a place of lower concentration in the air space. If using Kordon Breathing Bags, you should fill the bag completely with water, because these bags are permeable to carbon dioxide and oxygen, but only when the water is in contact with the plastic.

Improper Feeding

If your fish are not fat and active, perhaps their diet is to blame. Foods with a grain base (oats, corn, wheat, rice) may be good for you but not for insectivorous bettas. Grains have little nutritive value, are poorly digested, may block the intestine, cause starvation, force white mucus strands from the vent as the intestinal epithelium fails, and result in thin, weak fish. Switching to meaty live foods will restore health.

Infectious Diseases

Wild bettas are often infested with protozoa, bacteria, and worm parasites, and sometimes with crustacean parasites. Many of these parasites do little or no harm because wild fish have a balanced diet and good water quality, and parasites are few and far between, so their numbers on any fish are never great. The danger of introducing wild fish (or wild live food) is the introduction of their parasites. When parasites meet stressed fish in a confined space, disease may be the outcome.

The Immune System

Healthy fish can resist common diseases because their immune system attacks the disease agents. When fish are stressed, the immune system fails and the parasites may prevail.

In home aquariums, confined, crowded fishes are always stressed, and their immune system does not operate at full capacity. Lights switch on and off suddenly. Water is fouled by concentrated metabolic wastes rather than refreshed by flowing streams and regular rains. In the home aquarium, stressed bettas are susceptible to invading viruses, bacteria, and protozoa introduced with new fishes or water from pet stores, and sometimes microbes that were in the water all along.

The immune system is complex. The main point is that fishes cannot mobilize an initial immune response in cold water. That is why bettas should be maintained at temperatures similar to conditions in the wild. Lowland swamp bettas are accustomed to warm water (80–90°F [27–32°C] in open areas, cooler in forests), and upland stream bettas to cool temperatures (65–78°F [18–26°C]). Conditions that depress the immune system and place the fish at risk include low temperature, dietary deficiencies, low oxygen, and high carbon dioxide, nitrate, nitrite, or ammonia concentrations (exacerbated by high pH).

Viruses

Fish viruses have been studied extensively in fish grown for food or sport, but rarely in aquarium fishes. Viruses have no organs or capabilities of their own. They consist only of DNA or RNA and a protein shell with which they lock onto a fish cell. Once locked, the virus DNA or RNA squeezes out of its protein shell and into the host cell where it attaches to the host's DNA and takes over the protein-making machinery. Thereafter, the host makes only viruses until it dies. Sometimes these viruses can be seen with the electron microscope as particles, and sometimes as crystalline arrays of particles. These progeny viruses are extruded and the cell dies, but not always. The viruses then go on to infect other cells.

Viruses from wild fish can be transmitted from seemingly normal and even unrelated fishes. In a laboratory they are detected by clearings (plaques) in layers of fish cells. Those clearings are empty spaces where the viruses have killed the cells and they have exploded. Some viruses are always pathogenic. Other viruses become pathogenic in stressed fishes. Many viruses attack a wide variety of species, stressed or not. What can we do about them?

Antiviral drugs work by interfering with viral attachment to the host cell, or by blocking the production of new DNA or RNA. No antiviral drugs are yet approved or available for use in aquarium fishes. All we can do is avoid infections by use of quarantine, and minimize stresses from all causes.

Lymphocystis

Lymphocystis is an iridovirus that infects many kinds of fishes stressed by capture or shipping. It has no host specificity. Uncommon in the wild, it is common in captured marine fishes, and known from freshwater fishes in public aquariums. Strawberry-like lumps on the body and (mostly) the fins are clusters of invaded cells enlarged many times normal diameter (cytomegaly). The infection is rarely fatal, with the vastly swollen cells eventually resorbing back to normal size.

Systemic Iridovirus

Systemic iridovirus produces fatal cytomegaly that starts out resembling lymphocystis. Because nonfatal lymphocystis infects all kinds of fishes, systemic iridovirus, recently discovered in *Pterophyllum* (angelfish), might be similar and infect *Betta* and other anabantoids. If strawberry-like lumps are discovered, quarantine the entire aquarium and contact a fish pathologist at a veterinary school. The six-sided virus particles damage kidney cells, causing the accumulation of fluids in the body cavity (ascites) that makes the fish swell abnormally. The kidney damage also causes blood vessels behind the eyes to leak serum, causing the eyes to swell ("pop-eye" or exophthalmia). The mortality in angelfish may reach 70 percent, and there is no treatment, making this a potentially serious virus.

IPN

Infectious pancreatic necrosis (IPN) is a contagious, fatal virus disease infecting many kinds of fishes independently of stress. The pancreas is destroyed, and the fish invariably dies of metabolic failure. Infections of the pancreas can only be diagnosed by a veterinary pathologist. There is no cure.

Responding to an Outbreak

Because there are no approved medications to treat fish virus diseases, the only approach is to destroy all infected fish and any other fish with which they have come in contact. Decontaminate tanks, nets, and instruments with chlorine bleach. Use rubber gloves while working to prevent bleach burns and to avoid transmitting the viruses with contaminated water on your hands or tools.

Prevention

Ultraviolet (UV) disinfection destroys viral DNA and RNA and reduces the numbers of live viruses and bacteria. UV is used in public aquariums, large pet shops, private and commercial breeding facilities, and fish laboratories. UV units are available from pet shops and mail order sources at reasonable prices. The bulbs should be changed twice a year, and the tank water should be filtered before entering the UV exposure chamber. UV inactivation (by destroying DNA and RNA) is most effective in clear water (filtered water doesn't contain particles of silt that shade and protect viruses). Other

UV effectiveness factors are distance from the UV bulb (the closer the better), the emission intensity (higher energy, narrow short-wave bulbs are more effective than low-energy, long-wave bulbs), the type of bulb (wide-spectrum bulbs are more cost-effective than narrow-spectrum, high-energy bulbs), longer contact time (exposure time to the UV light during a pass through the sterilizer), and age of the bulb (emission intensity falls off, with bulbs good for about 6 months). UV-irradiated water should not be exposed to bright light for at least 20 minutes, because intense regular light can reverse UV damage by inducing DNA repair.

The new spiral path UV units give better uniformity of exposure to water passing through the UV chamber, so fewer viruses are shaded or missed. Do not use strong water pumps for UV units, because they force the water through too rapidly, reducing contact time.

Bacteria

There are 35 major groups of bacteria, from giants associated with deep sea vents to specialized forms related to fungi. The blue-green "algae" or cyanobacteria are in between bacteria and algae. Most aquarium bacteria are useful, from those in fish intestines that make vitamins to those that oxidize waste ammonia to nitrites and nitrates in the nitrogen cycle. Bacteria may be aerobic (requiring oxygen), anaerobic (requiring the absence of oxygen), or microaerophilic (adapted to reduced oxygen concentrations). They may require these conditions (obligate) or do just fine with or without these conditions (facultative). Many bacteria have flagella or cilia with which they swim (motile), and some have dense carbohydrate capsules that protect them from drugs and the immune system.

Some bacteria cause disease in stressed fishes, others in any fishes, some require a large dose to initiate infection, and others only a few microbes. The most invasive and damaging cause rapid fatalities in many fishes, with just a few bacteria sufficient to begin an outbreak. Often a water change and improved conditions can end an epidemic by allowing the fish's immune system to recover. With the severe bacteria, easy solutions will get you nowhere.

Diagnosis

We have treatments for three groups of bacteria. Selecting a treatment requires knowing which group caused the disease. Two of the groups can be identified through the Gram stain procedure. Here, a culture of bacteria is smeared onto a glass slide and dried. Then the slide is washed with a series of stains and solvents. At the end of the procedure (which only takes a few minutes) the bacteria appear red or purple. A red color is a gram-negative reaction. A purple color is a gram-positive reaction. The reactions reveal the nature of the bacterial cell wall. That's the key. We have antibiotics that can pass through and disrupt the cell walls from gram-negative (red) bacteria but not gram-positive (purple) bacteria, and vice versa. Antibiotics such as penicillin and streptomycin affect only gram-positive bacteria, and erythromycin mostly gram-positive bacteria. Tetracycline affects only gram-negative bacteria. Antibiotics that work on both kinds are called wide-spectrum antibiotics. Bacteria are also classified by size and shape (coccus or round, spiral, or a curved or straight, long or short rod); by whether they occur as individuals or collections (singles, doubles, strings of bacteria in a row, sheets, clusters of bacteria); by characteristics of a colony when cultured (smooth and shiny, rough and dull, special colors); and by their metabolism (ability to metabolize specific kinds of sugars, amino acids, and other compounds; ability to reduce iron, gases produced, or specific waste products; or ability to grow on specialized media).

Antibiotics and Antimicrobials

Chemicals synthesized in the laboratory (such as sulfa drugs) are called antimicrobials. Chemicals produced by other bacteria or fungi are called antibiotics. The fungus *Penicillium* produces the antibiotic penicillin, and the fungus *Strepto-*

myces makes the antibiotic streptomycin. Some antibiotics and antimicrobials can be put in the water, whereas others must be delivered in food to get inside the gut, the blood, or lymph. Still others must be injected. The route of delivery is important to aquarists.

Sulfa drugs are synthetic antimicrobials. Mixes of three different sulfas are popular medications, but are more effective when combined with an antibiotic. Many medications offer combinations.

Several dyes are marketed for disease control, but few are effective on bacteria. Methylene blue is a phloxine dye of little or no value as an antimicrobial. Phloxine B is an effective antiprotozoan agent when activated by bright light, but of no value against bacteria. Malachite green is an effective antiprotoan drug, but is ineffective against bacteria; it is toxic to fry and some adult fish at high concentrations. Acriflavines are mixtures of flavin dyes effective against bacteria in water. Acriflavin can damage larval fish DNA and kill fish eggs at high concentrations. Acriflavines can retard fungi, but do not have a track record against infectious bacteria. Methyl green is occasionally included in fish medications but its effectiveness has not been proven.

Oxytetracycline is an antibiotic effective against the important gram-negative bacteria *Aeromonas* and *Flexibacter*. Nifurpirinol, a synthetic furan drug (Furanace®, Furazolidone®) is effective against gram-negative bacteria. It is absorbed from water, but cannot be used in food because it decomposes when wetted in food, and also has an objectionable flavor to fishes. One dose of 2 mg/gal for 6 hours may be sufficient, but a second dose is better. Treat the fish in the dark, because the drug breaks down in bright light.

The antibiotic erythromycin works on gram-positive bacteria and is mildly effective on some gram-negative bacteria. It is seldom the drug of choice for aquarium fish because there are no important gram-positive pathogens. Its popularity in the hobby can be attributed to effective marketing.

The quinolones (oxolinic acid derivatives) are broad-spectrum antimicrobials effective against gram-positive and gram-negative bacteria, and can be applied in water, in food, or by injection of large fish. Do not use it directly in the aquarium, because it can kill nitrogen cycle bacteria in the gravel and filters. Treat the fish in a bath in a bare container. A new quinolone (enrofloxacin) kills gram-positive and gram-negative bacteria in blood and other tissues, and even inside fish cells. It is effective even at low concentrations and is nontoxic to fish.

Principal Bacterial Diseases

Septicemia and Gangrene

Blood poisoning (septicemia) is a bacterial infection of the bloodstream. Bacteria in the blood and lymph spread through the organs, shutting down the kidneys and interfering with osmotic balance. Symptoms of septicemia may be listlessness, exophthalmia ("pop eye"), and swelling (dropsy). The symptoms are caused by an accumulation of water in the tissues because the fish cannot pump it out. Other symptoms include ulcers, boils, wounds, or necrotizing tissue that seems to rot away. Internal abscesses may develop in liver and kidneys.

Edwardsiella ictaluri and *E. tarda* are the most common causes of lethal blood poisoning in all kinds of warm-water fishes. The recommended treatment for this and other gram-negative microbes is 3 grams of oxytetracycline in 100 pounds (45 kg) of food. Get medicated food from a veterinarian. Pet stores commonly keep medications beyond their expiration date.

Columnaris or Cotton Wool Disease

Cotton wool disease is caused by *Flexibacter (Cytophaga) columnaris,* one of the gram-negative bacteria that form yellow colonies in the laboratory. *Flexibacter* and the related *Flavobacterium* are especially pathogenic to *Betta* species. Initial symptoms might be hovering at the surface, gasping or coughing. Then you might see a translucent patch on the body that expands and ulcerates to expose bloody muscle beneath the decaying skin. Later mucus-like filaments of pure bacteria stream from body wounds and gills. The gill epithelium cells fuse and swell and the fish loses the ability to osmoregulate. It usually dies in less than 48 hours.

Stopping an outbreak of cotton wool disease requires isolating the fish and destroying any with advanced (bloody and wispy) lesions. Fishes with early stage translucent patches should be transferred to clean water with 4 teaspoons of salt to the gallon, and potassium chromate or potassium permanganate according to package directions. The salt assists osmotic balance and the permanganate oxidizes and kills the bacteria. Uninfected fish from the outbreak tank should be treated prophylactically with a nitrofuran bath to catch the disease before it is apparent. BettaMax, produced by Aquatronics, contains nitrofurazone and three sulfa drugs. The nitrofurazone is probably effective, but sulfas must be delivered in food or applied directly to a wound, and are not absorbed from water. A promising development is a vaccine made from the harmless bacterium *Flexibacter* (*Cytophaga*) *freundii*. The vaccine may confer immunity to this common fish disease.

Ulcerative Necrosis

The genus *Vibrio* contains the bent rod or comma-shaped bacteria that cause human cholera (*Vibrio comma*). *Vibrio marinum, V. anguillarum, V. ordali, V. damsela,* and related bacteria produce bloody wounds in the mouth, on the skin, around the eye, or internally in mus-

cles. Skin wounds appear as a black ring surrounding a white ring, with a hole in the center. The ulcers are deep and pale because red blood cells are liquefied by toxin so the vibrios can absorb their iron.

Vibrio vulnificans is devastating to humans with cirrhosis of the liver or depressed immune systems. They can die after eating raw oysters that concentrate this common marine bacterial species. Skin cuts in fishermen and divers also become infected, rapidly destroying the tissues so fast that amputation is the only way to stop the infection.

For a fish outbreak, the only treatment is a gram-negative specific antibiotic in the food, but it seldom works because infected fish typically stop eating. Oxytetracycline, oxolinic acid, and sulfonamides all work, but the best control is to prevent an outbreak through water changes, avoidance of crowding, swift removal of fish with symptoms, and sterilization of the aquarium with bleach if you get a full-blown outbreak.

Hemorrhagic Septicemia

Ulcers with black and white rings can be caused by *Aeromonas hydrophila, A. sobria, A. caviae*, or *Pseudomonas* species. These gram-negative short rods are normally found in all aquariums. These ulcers are shallow and bloody, rather than deep and pale as in vibrios.

Medicated foods (oxytetracycline, nifurpirinol, chloramphenicol) help, as does injecting the fish's abdomen with kanamycin. Most *Aeromonas* and *Pseudomonas* bacteria are harmless. Outbreaks occur when a plasmid (transferable gene) for pathogenicity is introduced into these bacteria from unrelated bacteria.

Fin and Tail Rot

Fin and tail rot may be caused by *Aeromonas* and *Pseudomonas* in fishes stressed by crowding, decomposing food in the aquarium, or fluctuating temperatures. The fins become brown or darkened at their eroded margins. Change water, add Melafix and one teaspoonful of marine salts per 5 gallons (19 L), do not feed any dry foods, increase aeration, reduce the light, and raise the temperature to about 85°F (29°C). Potassium permanganate sometimes helps, but may burn (oxidize) the gills. A 25-percent water change with *underchlorinated* tap water may help, because mild chlorine exposure can lower the microbe population without reaching a toxic level to fish. Don't try this in the summer when tap water is likely to contain chloramines.

"Pop Eye"

"Pop eye," or exophthalmos, without septicemia indicates a localized bacterial infection of the sinuses. The bacteria in the epithelial linings in the head produce gases that force the eyeball outward. The only treatment is gram-negative antibiotics in food, and it doesn't always work. Many kinds of bacteria produce gas, and most can reach the eye if infections proceed to septicemia. If the fish doesn't die within a week, it is likely to live.

Acid-Fast Disease, Fish Tuberculosis, Fish-Tank Finger

The acid-fast staining procedure is used in laboratories to detect bacteria that cause tuberculosis and leprosy. These "acid-fast" bacteria have wax-laden cell walls resistant to the antibiotics that destroy gram-negative and gram-positive bacteria. Acid-fast bacteria also grow slowly, so specialized medications must be used for a long period to work. Medications are available for treating human diseases, but not those of fishes. The most common acid-fast bacteria of *Betta* are *Mycobacterium marinum* (= *Mycobacterium anabanti, Mycobacterium piscium*) and *Mycobacterium ulcerans.* These acid-fast infections are common in fishes with impaired immune systems caused by stress or age. Infected fish develop hollow bellies, slowly developing bloody lesions. The organs are filled with walled off aggregations of live and dead white blood cells surrounding clumps of bacteria, and are called granulomas (easily seen under a microscope). Diagnosis is confirmed by a positive (red) acid-fast stain procedure. There are no cost-effective treatments, and affected fish are removed or quarantined until they die.

Acid-fast bacteria are not very contagious to other fishes, but they can sometimes infect humans when hands with bleeding cuts are immersed in aquariums. The disease also occurs in swimmers with cuts, because these bacteria are everywhere. A slowly developing sore that does not heal, anywhere on the body but especially the hands, should be examined by a physician for *Mycobacterium marinum*. Advise the physician of *www.cabipublishing.org/bookshop/readingroom/0851991947/1947ch9.pdf*. It is treatable in humans, but a full cure may take months.

Protozoa

Velvet

Piscinoodinium causes velvet disease in fishes. It is a member of the dinoflagellates, a group claimed by both botanists and zoologists. At least two species infest aquarium fishes. Reports of velvet with chloroplasts and those without perhaps correspond to these species. *Piscinoodinium* of tropical fishes is closely related to *Gymnodinium*, the alga that causes red tide.

Velvet flourishes where water quality has declined. It is the single most important killer of fry of *Betta splendens,* and it is common in adult bettas. When uneaten food is decomposed, the bacteria emit toxins, release wastes, and consume oxygen. Fish have difficulty breathing or resisting infection. In baby tanks especially, the fry are easy prey for *Piscinoodinium,* which is always around. The dinoflagellate can be spread from tank to tank through mists created by aeration. In adult fish, the infection looks like a dusty, dark golden layer over the body and eyes when you shine a flashlight at an angle to their flanks.

Piscinoodinium invades epithelium and sucks up body fluids for nutrition. A healthy adult can withstand a heavy infection for weeks, but fry cannot survive for long. *Piscinoodinium* in adult fish is treated with copper sulfate or formalin, but killing parasites (which fall away from the skin) leaves open wounds that are quickly invaded by bacteria that normally are noninvasive. They cause a blood infection leading to kidney failure, ultimately leading to swelling and death. The disease is eliminated but the patient dies.

Velvet is more easily controlled than treated. Velvet can be kept at bay by maintaining good water quality (siphoning decaying food from the bottom of the fry tank) and a salt concentration of 1 teaspoon of salt per 1 gallon (4 L) of water to assist osmotic balance. If fry are infected, most will be lost and the few survivors so weakened as to develop poorly, often stunted, and sometimes deformed.

White Spot, or Ich

The most common protozoan disease of tropical fish is infection by *Ichthyophthirius multifilis*. This parasitic ciliated protozoan is everywhere in natural waters and causes epidemics when fishes are stressed and immune defenses are lowered by cold temperatures. Ich is a common springtime disease of pond fishes

Immunity

People and fishes resist disease in several ways. The first barrier is the acidic skin that discourages bacterial invasion. A second barrier is the immune system, consisting of two kinds of protection, cellular and humoral. Cellular immunity is provided by specialized white blood cells attached to filtering organs like the liver, or wandering freely about inside and outside the blood and lymph vessels. All these white blood cells engulf foreign materials (bacteria, viruses, fungi, dead tissues) and digest them. These white blood cells, or phagocytes (phago = eat, cyto = cell), concentrate at wounds and we see them as pus.

The humoral substances (humoral = blood) are the antibodies and cell-killing substances (cytokinins). When the body detects a foreign protein, specialized white blood cells (not phagocytes) rearrange their DNA and divide, then emit specific substances (antibodies) that immobilize, bind, or wrap up the foreign protein to make it susceptible to gobbling phagocytes. If the host fish has never before seen this foreign protein (usually the surface of a microbe), its response is slow and the microbe might destroy the fish before an adequate response can be mobilized. If, on the other hand, this is the second time that microbe has invaded, then the host quickly produces massive amounts of antibody.

The success of the immune response depends on temperature and the general health of the fish. The initial and all later immune responses work better at elevated temperatures. The initial response that arms the fish against future attacks fails at low temperatures.

and, because many aquarium fishes are produced in ponds in Florida, it is common in pet stores in spring. In aquariums it is always around, probably persisting at levels too low to detect (one or two spots on one of the fish). Stress or the introduction of a new fish can trigger an outbreak. Fish that recover from ich develop immunity and seldom become seriously infected again, but they can be carriers. The most frequent cause of ich is introduction of a new pet store fish (and its bag water) during spring. The ich spores can also be transmitted with siphons, nets, and wet hands from tank to tank.

The disease first appears as a few white spots on the body or fins. After several days, the number and the size of the spots increase dramatically. In the parasite life cycle, a young swimming protozoan penetrates the skin and grows until it reaches a large size. This feeding stage, or trophont (troph = to feed), in the skin is the white spot, and it may grow to the size of a pinhead. At maturity, the trophont forms a cyst around itself and breaks out of the skin, where it drifts until it sticks to the gravel, rocks, or plants. The stage inside the cyst, called a tomont, divides repeatedly to produce up to a thousand offspring called theronts. When fully developed, these theronts break out of the cyst and swim about seeking to infect more fish. Crowded fish are easily found and invaded. Once the theronts burrow into the skin, they become feeding trophonts and the cycle continues.

Protected by the fish's skin, the protozoan is protected from chemicals. Within its cyst, it is protected from chemicals. Only when the infective stage breaks out and swims through the water is ich susceptible to treatment with formalin, malachite green, or copper sulfate. Treatment should be prolonged to catch theronts as they break out of cysts. Raise the aquarium temperature to speed up the parasite life cycle and boost the fishes' immune systems. Experimental tests of ich vaccines are being investigated, based on exposing the fish to related but harmless protozoans that may confer a cross-immunity.

Costia

Costia, or *Ichyobodo natrix,* is a flagellated protozoan that swarms over the skin of bettas and causes skin blotches, discoloration, and fin erosion. As the parasites feed, they cause the fish to scratch against hard surfaces, leading to abrasions likely to become infected with bacteria. Treat with a formalin dip (four to six drops of 37–40 percent formaldehyde solution per gallon) in a separate container until the fish show distress (and then change water), a full strength sea water bath for 30 minutes, or two drops per gallon of a 0.75 percent malachite green solution. Sometimes just adding rock salt or marine salts (but not iodized salt) to the aquarium will cause *Costia* to die off.

Chilodonella

These highly pathogenic protozoans invade skin and gills where they do considerable damage. *Chilodonella* multiply by continuous simple division across the middle. It's a scourge of fish farms, hatcheries, and aquariums, sometimes covering fishes in a solid layer. The individual parasites are small and difficult to see without a microscope.

Chilodonella has hard parts around its cytostome (mouth) that scrape skin and gill tissues, destroying them, and feeding on the necrotic cell debris. In gills, it also triggers surviving cells to proliferate (hyperplasia), which is followed by white blood cell invasion, capillary enlargement and rupture, hemorrhaging, and death by bleeding. Because there are no obvious signs, such as big white spots, the disease is often too advanced to treat. The best medicine is a formalin dip, but *Chilodonella* forms cysts that remain

Two male Betta splendens *in combat.*

in the aquarium long after the disease has disappeared, so it can reappear at any time.

Tetrahymena

Tetrahymena grow as diffuse white patches on the body or eye. The fish swell and the scales stick out as in dropsy, and there may be fin and tail rot. Other damage is produced internally. A skin or head scraping placed in water under the microscope will reveal tiny parasites spiraling through the water, rather than traveling in a straight line. Of several species, some form long-lasting cysts. *Tetrahymena* invade skin, gills, muscle, and organs, where they scrape and destroy the tissues they then engulf as food. They multiply like ich, with cysts hatching to release multiple invasive offspring. Formalin is effective.

Glugea

Glugea is an infectious internal protozoan that multiplies by long-lasting cysts. When the fish dies or is eaten, the cysts are liberated, and survive for weeks to years in sediments. There are many known species, and they may be host specific to anabantoids and other groups. *Glugea* infections start as small white pimple-like eruptions on the skin, and grow and multiply while the host becomes lethargic, thin, and stops feeding. Death is inevitable, and the disease is contagious. The only control is to destroy all fishes and plants in the tank, and sterilize the tank and rocks with bleach.

Gill and Skin Flukes

Gill and skin flukes are external flatworm parasites (monogenea) with translucent bodies and clamps or hooks at one end. The flukes graze on epithelial tissue, and in captive fish, large numbers can create severe irritations that become infected with bacteria. Gill and skin flukes generally produce fertilized eggs, but a few are live-bearers. The eggs of some species sink to the bottom, and those of other species have entangling filaments that give them lift in the water and wrap around fish gills. The egg hatches into a ciliated larva that finds and attaches to a host fish, transforms into an adult, and finds a mate on that same fish, and then the two fertilize each other's eggs. It's a simple life cycle with no intermediate host.

When fish are crowded, infestation rates can be heavy. Any wild-caught fish might have some flukes on its gills or skin, but these readily spread to adjacent fishes in crowded conditions. With high numbers of parasites per fish, gill irritation, erosion, and heavy bleeding affect breathing, and provide wounds for invasive bacteria and fungi that get to the bloodstream and cause overwhelming septicemia. Outbreaks are common in hatcheries and at fish import facilities, and can occur in densely stocked tanks.

A common treatment is dilute formalin using 4 drops per 1 gallon (4 L) (in a separate bare aquarium or jar) with strong aeration. Then add 1 drop per gallon per hour more until the fish become distressed. At this point, change 50 percent of the water and continue aeration for at least 24 hours. Many public aquariums use a 5-minute dip in full-strength marine water for any freshwater fish, and vice versa. Still another treatment is the organophosphate trichlorfon (Dylox, Dipterex, Masoten, Negavon) at 2–5 mg/L for 60 minutes, but it is pH sensitive, breaks down quickly in warm water, and may be difficult to find. Benzocaine may get the worms to relax their grips and fall away. Copper sulfate is not very effective.

Internal Flukes and Tapeworms

Wild bettas may carry internal flukes in any part of the body or tapeworms in the intestine. Neither kind of worm can be transmitted from fish to fish in aquariums, nor do they cause epidemics. Equally important, they are not pathogens, but a normal part of life in the wild. Healthy wild fishes can support substantial parasite loads. Treatment serves no purpose, and may cause stress.

Nematodes

The only nematode worm common in aquarium fishes is *Camallanus*, a (usually) pink or red intestinal worm usually infecting pond fishes, and capable of doing damage to bettas when they are abundant. *Camallanus* is spread by intermediate copepod hosts. Diagnosis is by observation of multiple pink or red hairlike extrusions from the anus of the fish. Treat with the veterinary drug flubendazole (Panacur) in water or food. Other nematocidal drugs used for dog and cat infections are available from veterinarians as canned medicated foods that you can feed to fishes.

Arthropod Parasites

Arthropod parasites occur on wild fish but are not problematic in tank-raised bettas. The most common arthropod on wild mouthbrooding bettas (or any anabantoid) are fish lice (*Argulus, Dolops*). Aquarium or pond organophosphates are used to treat fish lice in hatcheries, but for home aquarists it is simpler to remove the parasite with tweezers while holding the fish in a net and wet handkerchief. Other, smaller parasitic copepods that may occur on

gills respond to formalin or marine water dips. Large lernaeid copepods (anchor worms) may embed in the flesh of larger anabantoids including mouthbrooders. They cannot be pulled out. These fish should be quarantined or discarded, as killing the parasite (half inside and half outside) with organophosphates risks a dead, decaying parasite inside the fish's body (sometimes its heart).

General Considerations

Your fish are more valuable than the money you paid for them. They may have cost enormous efforts for acquisition, breeding, and raising. Experimenting with medications in the absence of a rational diagnosis wastes time and money and perhaps the lives of your fishes. The best course is to carry your fish (by appointment) to a veterinary school or veterinarian specializing in fish diseases for a diagnosis and the appropriate drug. Your local pet dealer may be a nice enough fellow, but he isn't a pathologist.

Chapter Seven

Zoogeography 101 – Where Bettas Live and How They Got There

Bettas are modern fishes (Perco-morphs, Anabantoids) whose distribution has been affected by ice ages that caused the rise and fall of sea levels. Anabantoids in nature range from western and southern Africa to China and southward to Indonesia, but they do not extend to Australia and New Guinea.

Betta History

Ancestral anabantoids populated both Africa and Asia, and their modern derived species occur on both continents today, although the two continents no longer share any genera. Most anabantoids are generalists that eat insects and live in the tropics. Some are specialized, and may have changed little over the eons. *Helostoma* (kissing gouramies) and *Osphronemus* (giant gouramies) are primitive forms that have changed little. *Helostoma* is a specialized filter feeder (it has many fine gill rakers for sieving plankton), and *Osphronemus* is a fruit and seed eater much like *Colossoma* of the Amazon River in South America. *Sandelia* is uniquely adapted to the cold temperate climate of South Africa.

Recently evolved anabantoids, such as *Betta* and *Parosphromenus,* spread throughout what is now Indonesia and Malaysia during the Pleistocene Ice Age, when the Earth was a few degrees colder, large amounts of water were tied up as polar ice, and sea levels were far lower. Now that the planet is in a warm phase, the ice caps have mostly melted and sea levels are higher.

Because anabantoids are not salt-tolerant, they could not have gotten to so many islands by island hopping. They had to get there before these lands were islands, when the (present) islands were the highland on a single land mass. Harold Voris and Till

How Evolution Works

The larger a population, the more mutations it accumulates over time, and the more its DNA varies among individuals. Species slowly come into existence when a portion of the general population is cut off, and it loses much of its genetic diversity. The remaining genes become more frequent in the population, and new genes appear that are restricted to this cut-off population. Eventually, the cut-off population is so genetically different that it is unable to interbreed with its ancestral group. It will often develop distinctive markings or shapes or teeth or fin rays and body proportions. Some genetic traits that become fixed and characterize the newly evolved form are random and of no particular survival value (color patterns), whereas others are nonrandom and of significant selective value (teeth adapted to a new food source). When the isolated population can no longer reasonably be expected to interbreed successfully with the ances-tral population, the isolated population is considered a new species.

Where does speciation most often occur? In the Great Rift Valley lakes of Africa, it occurs in isolated lakes cut off from the Great Lake during long periods (eras) of drought, when the Great Lake is a series of disconnected small lakes. In the United States, it occurs in the uppermost tributaries of great rivers, where a crow-flies distance between two upper tributaries might be 1 mile (1.5 km), but the river distance (downstream and then back upstream where the tributaries meet) might be 1,000 miles (1,609 km).

In the case of *Betta*, speciation occurred when the ancient population was broken into multiple isolated populations as rising sea levels cut off all the Sunda River's tributaries from each other, with only the uppermost tributary populations surviving to this day on different islands (hilltops of the ancient basin).

Hanebuth provided maps of the Sunda Shelf and the Sahil Shelf, two different land masses that were exposed during the low sea levels during the Pleistocene Ice Age. Based on the maps, you can see how *Betta* spread to its current locations but was unable to go any farther.

During the later Pleistocene, the area we now know as Indochina, Malaysia, and Indonesia, including Borneo, were all a single land mass drained by one giant river, the ancient Sunda. The Sunda emptied to the northeast into a small bay that has since become the South China Sea. The spread and evolution of *Betta* (and *Parosphromenus*) occurred when the Sunda occupied that single land mass. Today, the

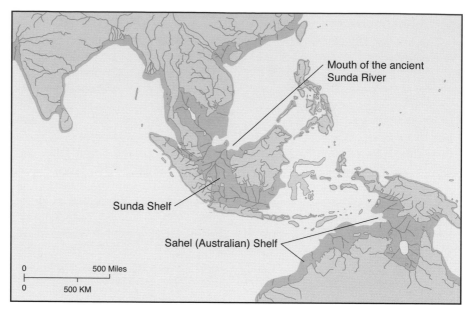

Southeast Asia 6,000–26,000 years ago (Ice Age). Shaded areas are the Sunda shelf and Sahel shelf.

Sunda River has been drowned by the rising ocean, and the species of *Betta* have been cut off from each other.

The ancient Sunda River was comparable in size to the Congo or the Amazon (Roberts, 1989). In large rivers, the fastest evolution occurs in the uppermost tributaries, tiny streams frequently isolated by perturbations in global temperature, drought, the rise and erosion of mountains, land subsidence, and other events that fracture populations.

The Sunda River was at its greatest when the Pleistocene Ice Age reached its peak 26,000 years ago. Sea levels were about 240 feet (73 m) lower, and other great rivers around the world emptied into lower oceans. Today, those ancient seashores at the edges of the continents are called the Continental Shelves. A warming period ended the Pleistocene's Great Ice Age and sea levels rose rapidly in spurts, much of it in the last 6,000 years, to today's level. As the oceans rose, the Sunda River was submerged by the rising sea, leaving its uplands isolated and still above sea level. Those isolated lands today are the Malay Peninsula, Sumatra, Java, Borneo, Bali, and smaller islands all sitting on that ancient lowland (now submerged) that we call the Sunda Shelf (Hanebuth et al., 2000; Voris, 2000).

The shallow Melaka Strait (= Molucca Strait) between the Malay Peninsula and Sumatra was a

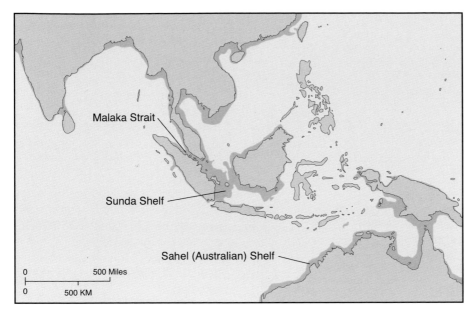

Southeast Asia today. Shaded areas are the Sunda shelf and Sahel shelf.

land bridge, as were the strait between Sumatra and Java, and the shallow sea bed between Java and Borneo. Other smaller islands (like Bangka Island off Sumatra) also sit on the shallow Sunda Shelf. Fishes could readily move across those land bridges through rivers, streams, and during floods.

With more than 20,000 years of isolation, many distinct species have evolved on the separated Sunda Islands, all in isolated river systems. A few primitive species survive in widely separated populations on such presently distant lands as the Malay Peninsula in the west and Borneo in the east. Those species must have evolved at least 6,000 years ago.

No anabantoid has reached the Philippines by hopping through the cluster of islands northeastward from Borneo. And no anabantoid has crossed the Makassar Strait between Borneo and Sulawesi. Farther south, no anabantoids have crossed from the Sunda Islands to New Guinea and Australia (on the Sahil Shelf).

Today's Sunda Sub-Region (the old Sunda River basin) of Asia has a distinctive Asian fauna (and not just the fishes). Biologists call this faunistic area Wallacea, after Henry Wallace, the naturalist who studied the fauna of the region at the same time Darwin was studying the fauna of South America.

Across the Makasar Strait to the east, the fauna becomes a mix of animals of Asian and Australian descent. Farther east we cross Lydekker's Line to the Australian faunistic area typical of the Sahil (Australian Shelf) where no anabantoids ever occurred.

This is how anabantoids dispersed, how they evolved, and how they were confined. We still don't know what exists in the interior of Borneo because of lack of roads. We know little about the anabantoids of Burma, in part because few biologists go there since the harsh military dictatorship took power. Sometimes even where we can go, it's smarter not to. The eastern (Timor) and western (Aceh) ends of Indonesia are dangerous because of warring separatist groups and the Indonesian army and local militias. The distribution of fishes, as we know it, depends on the distribution of ichthyologists. As scientists are able to travel to more places, we will learn more about where *Betta* species live, how they live, what they look like, and what new kinds of habitats they might occupy.

The Geography of Bettas

There are natural limits to the distribution of the genus *Betta*. Lower sea levels allowed them to spread southward from Thailand and Cambodia throughout the Sunda Islands between 26,000 and 6,000 years ago. Their movement north and east of the ancient Sunda River basin has been blocked by mountains. Some *Betta* species might have found their way into the surrounding areas through lowland valleys lying between mountains, so we must continue to explore fringe fingers of potential habitat.

Knowledge of the fishes of Cambodia is limited in part because of its recent political history (the terror of the Khmer Rouge) and the continuing dangers of working in that country. *B. splendens* and *B. prima* occur here and perhaps unknown species as well. Our knowledge is limited to western tributaries of the Mekong River, and what lies to the east is unknown.

Southern Vietnam is dominated by the broad floodplain of the Mekong River Delta, and this tropical region offers vast areas of habitat for species of *Betta*. Northern Vietnam is almost entirely mountainous north of the Tum Plateau near the border of Vietnam with Laos and Cambodia. The climate of northern Vietnam is also colder, and no species of *Betta* should be expected here. Kottelat's (2001) review of the fishes of northern Vietnam reports some anabantoids, but no species of *Betta*. Laos, which borders much of Vietnam, Thailand, and Cambodia to the north (Cummings, 1998), is thoroughly mountainous, offering no opportunities for the genus to spread into this forbidding land.

Where do bettas come from? Where were they or can they be collected? Good books on anabantoid fishes provide sufficient location information. Each report may list a town, a river basin, a road, or a province, or a distance along a road from point A to point B. If we were talking about American fishes, then you would know where the Mississippi River, Illinois, Texas, or Chicago was located, and it would be sufficient to say the fish was discovered there. However, Americans (and many Europeans) don't know the native lands of bettas nearly so well. For this reason, the following discussion will help you find on a map where in the world THAT place or THAT river (holding THAT betta) is located. For serious aquarists (or sneaky spouses) planning a combined vacation and collecting trip, it's important to know not only where to look but also whether to look at all. Finding fish is easier with good maps and good descriptions of where fish are found. Get the best maps available. I recommend the Nelles publishing company in Germany. The best travel guides are published by Lonely Planet. Contact the appropriate embassy and inquire of any laws or permits for collecting their native species. Often a colleague in that country or a contact with a university biologist can be helpful. Contact the U.S. Fish & Wildlife Service for a *Declaration for Importation or Exportation of Fish or Wildlife*. You may need to use a licensed U.S. importer working with a foreign exporter to get the fishes from there to here. Contact the U.S. Centers for Disease Control and Prevention (CDC) to learn which dis-

eases are endemic to the area, how to avoid them, what shots you should get, which diseases may be unavoidable, and whether special precautions are necessary. For example, you can take pills to prevent malaria, but not to prevent dengue fever. You can avoid schistosomiasis only by staying out of the water or by wearing boots and rubber gloves. Get a printout from the CDC and discuss it with your physician. What nets and equipment should you take? Often the best equipment is cash for the natives who will be happy to take the plunge with your nets and catch useless inedible bait for the foolish American. Breathing bags can hold packaged fishes for a week or more, and stackable plastic shoeboxes are ideal for holding them day to day and giving them water changes. Paper test kits provide information on water quality, and a handheld global positioning system tells you exactly where you are and, by extension, precisely at which river drainage. When you think you've planned well, put it all out on an aquarium chat room to refine the advice, get tips on places to search, and gather ideas you never thought about. You cannot plan too long or too well.

Thailand (Siam)

Thailand, the home of the Siamese fighting fish, is bordered to the north and east by Laos, to the west by Burma, and to the south by the Malay Peninsula in the west and

Thailand. The Korat Plateau is in the northeast.

the Gulf of Thailand to the east. The most northern point is Nong Khai, just south of Vientiane, Laos. The most important city is Bangkok on the Gulf of Thailand. Western Thailand is the upper portion of the Malay Peninsula (the lower portion is western Malaysia).

The center of Thailand is mostly rolling hills and valleys, with swampy lowlands along floodplains of the larger rivers. The Tanen Mountains dominate western Thailand, and the Louang and Phang Mountains are features of the far north. The Korat Plateau, home of

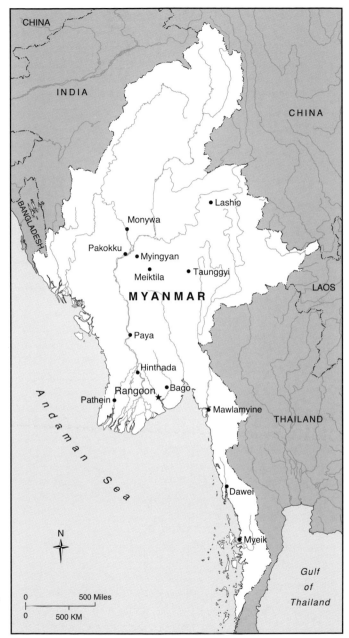

Burma (Myanmar).

Betta smaragdina, is an elevated plain in the northeast.

The streams arising in the mountains converge and drain the middle of the country, forming the Phraya River, which empties into the Gulf of Thailand at Bangkok. The far sides of the mountains drain toward Laos into the upper Mekong River, which then flows to Cambodia and Vietnam, emptying into the South China Sea. For more information see the Central Intelligence Agency (CIA) web site *(www.cia.gov/cia/publications/fact book/geos/th.html), The Lonely Planet Guide to Thailand,* (1999), and the 1:1,500,000 map published by Nelles Verlag, Munich, Germany.

The species of Thailand include *B. splendens, B. smaragdina, B. imbellis, B.* sp. Mahachai, *B. pugnax, B. prima,* and *B. pi.* The first four are bubblenesters and the last three are mouthbrooders. For continuous reports on the bettas of Thailand, search *www.siamensis.org.*

Burma

Burma is bordered by the Andaman Sea and the Indian Ocean, Thailand, China, and India. The major cities are Mandalay in the north and Rangoon (= Yangon) in the south.

The highest elevations are the Himalayas in the north. The lowest elevations are the coral reefs of the west coast. Most large rivers flow from the mountains southward and empty into the Gulf of Martaban (= Mottama) on the Andaman Sea, a corner of the Indian Ocean.

Burma or Myanmar?

The U.S. government considers Burma the official name. The military took power in a coup and never allowed the elected government to take power. The military changed the country's name to Myanmar, a change never approved by the elected legislature and never adopted by the United States.

The most southerly area is the mountain and lowland division of Tanintharyi (= Tenasserim). Just to the north is Kayin (= Karen) State. Kayin and Tanintharyi have extensive lowlands and are likely areas to have anabantoids. Kayah, north of Kayin, is too mountainous for anabantoids. Yangon Division west of Kayin and Bago Division to the north have extensive lowlands. Ayeyarwady Division to the west of Yangon has the vast Ayeyarwady Delta and a large river floodplain that could offer anabantoid habitat. The remaining areas north and west are mountainous and unlikely to have anabantoids.

The Lonely Planet Guide and the CIA web site provide information about visiting Burma and, in fact, Dr. Kottelat has recently published on a collection of fishes made here, indicating that (with government approval) scientists can still conduct work in the country.

Burma has *Colisa, Parasphaerichthys, Pseudosphromenus, Trichopsis,* and *Osphronemus.* Burma might have unknown *Betta*

Habitats of Malaysia and the Sunda Shelf

Dominant features are volcanic mountains, coastal mangrove swamps, and peat-forest swamps. The volcanic mountain lakes are not important *Betta* habitats, although other fishes live there.

Coastal mangrove swamps, extensive on Borneo and eastern Sumatra, are defined by variable salinity, coastal soils, and the mangroves *Avicennia, Rhizophora, Sonneratia, Nypa,* and *Bruguiera*. The lowest salinity areas are dominated by *Nypa* palms, and *Betta* species sometimes occur here. In mangrove areas, productivity is based on decomposition of mangrove leaf litter, and the most important food sources for fishes are falling mangrove ants and mites.

The strangest habitats are ancient swamp-forest pools and seeps. Eons of rainfall, shade, high humidity, low temperatures, and anaerobic decomposition of fallen hardwood leaves produce wetland soils called histosoils that have changed into peat. Tropical peat histosoils are too deep for plant roots to reach the underlying mineral-laden soils. Endless rainfall leaches nutrients from tropical histosoils, and the overlying embedded forests become stunted. Stunted swamp forests are typical habitats of the *Betta coccina* and *Betta waseri* species groups.

The typical *Betta* species of these strange habitats are the *waseri* and *coccina* groups, fish that feed mostly on ants and mites. Perhaps the red pigment of forest floor *Betta coccina* group species is poster coloration like that of South American dart frogs that also occupy forest floors. Perhaps, like dart frogs, the red *Betta coccina* complex accumulates toxins from ants that make them distasteful or poisonous to predators. That's a subject for a graduate thesis.

species, but there are no reports other than a record of *B. splendens* that is probably an introduction.

Western Malaysia (Malay Peninsula)

Western Malaysia occupies the southern portion of the Malay Peninsula, just south of Thailand. Singapore is an independent state at its southern tip, a ferry ride away. Western Malaysia contains mountain ranges, lowland rain forests, and great rivers, some dammed for reservoirs to provide hydroelectric power. The provinces of Western Malaysia are Perlis, Kedah, Perak, Selangor, Pahang, Negeri Sembilan, Melaka, and Johore. See the map for the locations of cities and rivers.

For more information on Western Malaysia, see the CIA web site *(www.cia.gov/cia/publications/fact book/geos/my.html)* and the map

Western Malaysia (Malay Peninsula) and Singapore.

published by Nelles Verlag, Munich, Germany.

Species reported from Western Malaysia include *B. bellica, B. taeniata,* and *B. hipposideros.*

Singapore

Singapore is on a delta of the Johore River at the southern tip of the Malay Peninsula. Lim and Ng's (1990) guidebook to the freshwater fishes of Singapore is inexpensive at $5, but shipping to the United States from the Singapore Science Center requires an additional cost

for postage. Bintan Island off the coast of Singapore has ancient peat-swamp forest habitat, similar to the habitat that was lost with the burgeoning growth of Singapore.

Some 95 percent of Singapore's habitat has been lost in the past 183 years (Brock et al., 2003), along with it local extinctions of fishes, butterflies, birds, and mammals (34–87 percent), and amphibians, reptiles, plants, crustaceans, and other creatures (5–80 percent). Singapore's remaining forest reserves take up one-fourth of 1 percent of the land area, yet support half the remaining biodiversity. At this rate of habitat loss, Brock et al. predicted the loss of 13–42 percent of the populations in the next 100 years, of which half will be total extinctions.

Species reported from Singapore include *B. taeniata, B. pugnax, B. tomi* (extirpated); the species *B. miniopinna* may survive on Bintan Island.

Indonesia

Indonesia is 3,000 miles (5,000 km) from east to west along the equator, and 1,000 miles (1,700 km) north and south. Its 13,000 islands sit among tropical reefs and support snow-capped mountains. It was the land of the spice trade fought over by the British, Dutch, and Portuguese. Today Indonesia is making great strides toward democracy under the eyes of the entrenched military. A secular nation of myriad religious factions, it recently made peace with separatists in the east, but is still fighting with separatists in the west.

Indonesia's major political areas are the islands of Sumatra, Java, Bali, and most of Borneo (of which Kalimantan is Indonesian and the northern portion is Malaysian), and the smaller island groups of Nusa Tenggara, Sulawesi, Maluku, and the Bandas. Indonesia also includes the state of Irian Jaya on the west side of New Guinea.

Some of the typical flora and fauna of Indonesia include the giant Rafflesi flowers, the Komodo dragon, orchids and birds galore, many aquatic turtles, and impressive stands of hardwood timber. Much of the flora and fauna is protected by national parks, but effects of the pet trade (not just to the United States and Europe, but to China and Japan as well), plus harvest for food, folk medicine, and furniture has been devastating to certain regions, especially near population centers. Java, for example, is known to have only a single species of *Betta*.

A biological border called the Wallace Line running north and south from eastern Borneo through eastern Bali separates the Asian faunal province from the Australian-Pacific faunal province. *Betta* species with their Asian origin exist only west of this line, but not to the east. The great naturalist Alfred Russell Wallace was studying the flora and fauna in this part of the world at the same time Charles Darwin was studying the New World. Both men came up with the idea of evolution at the same time but Darwin, learning of Wallace's ideas, rushed to beat him into print and history. Were it not for Darwin's rush to publish while Wallace was still considering the congruence of both men's ideas, Darwin might have been a footnote to history and Wallace the father of evolution. Today, modern thought identifies another line (Lydekker's line) that shifts the Australian Pacific faunal line to New Guinea. In between, Sulawesi, Maluku, and Nussa Tengara are a faunal province of mixed origins.

Sumatra and Bangka Island, Indonesia.

The genus *Betta* spread to Indonesia from Indo-China during periods of low sea level, when Borneo, Java, and Sumatra were one contiguous land mass on a southeast Asia continental shelf exposed by falling sea levels. The genus did not spread farther eastward, because no land bridges were available to cross the deep sea floor.

To recognize map features of Indonesia and even to read technical articles and other aquarium books about anabantoids, you should know that "Sengai" means river, "Selat" is Strait, "Barat" is west, "Selatan" is south, "Timur" is east, "Utara" is north, "Tanjung" is a point or peninsula, "Desa" is village, "Pulau" means island, "Danau" is lake, "Gunung" is mountain, and "Gunug Api" is volcano.

Sumatra

Sumatra is the westernmost part of Indonesia. It is the elongate island just across the Strait of Melaka to the north. Sumatra, Borneo, Java, Bali, and the surrounding smaller islands sit upon the submerged Sunda (Asian) shelf. They were all connected in one continuous land mass when sea levels were lower and the Sunda shelf represented the edge of the sea. To see the shoreline of the past and the Sunda Shelf, click on *http://www.fmnh.org/research_collections/zoology/zoo_sites/seamaps/default.htm.*

Many islands surround Sumatra. They include Bangka in the northeast, Belitung in the Belitung island group east of Bangka, the Riau group off the east coast, the Mentawai islands off the west coast, and Nias, the largest of the western group.

Sumatra is west of Java, the two islands separated by the Sunda Strait. The most important feature of the Strait is Krakatoa volcano, mostly now hidden below the sea.

Java, Indonesia.

Krakatoa erupted in 1883 with a thunderous sound that could be heard 2,000 miles away in Australia, and it could erupt again tomorrow.

The entire region is geologically active, with regular earthquakes, tsunamis, and volcanic eruptions. Sumatra has about 100 volcanoes on its southern side. To the north, lowlands and brackish swamps face the Melaka Strait. The highest of many mountains and volcanoes is Mount Kerinci, at about 10,000 feet (3,000 m). The donut-shaped Lake Toba in the north surrounds its own central island like a moat. The east side of Sumatra is lowland and swamp. The west side is mountainous, but a narrow band of lowlands provides *Betta* habitat. Large lakes abound.

Betta species are usually located by river systems, provinces, and nearest towns, and are nicely illustrated on the Nelles 1:1,500,000 map of Sumatra (Nelles Verlag, Munich, Germany).

Betta species reported from Sumatra and its adjacent islands include *B. imbellis, B. bellica, B. coccina, B. miniopinna, B. chloropharynx, B. burdigala, B. edithae, B. falx, B. fusca, B. tomi, B. renata,* and *B. rubra.* There may be additional species, and some of the named populations may yet be shown to be new species.

Java

Java lies between Sumatra to the west and Bali to the east, separated from Sumatra by the Sunda Strait and from Bali by the Bali Strait. Sumatra, Bali, and Java comprise the Greater Sunda Islands.

Java is dominated by volcanoes in the south and lowlands in the north. The south drains to the Indian Ocean, and the north drains to lowlands and the Java Sea.

The Java Sea is dominated by drift currents that move slowly or not at all, and turbidity (silt) from rivers draining Java and Borneo. With a shallow shelf and little mixing and dilution, the silt remains suspended and higher than in the Indian Ocean in the same way that Mississippi River silt murks the ordinarily clean Gulf of Mexico. Despite the murk,

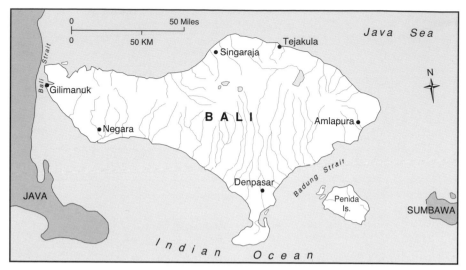
Bali, Indonesia.

coral reefs abound in the Java Sea northeast of Jakarta in the Thousand Islands (actually just 108 islands). Most of the rivers draining from the southern slopes of the mountains to the Indian Ocean are short and the alluvial lowland (Coastal Plain of Jakarta) is narrow.

Java is densely populated and highly developed. Despite the large population (120 million), many uplands remain in original forests. The lowlands have been altered for agriculture, but pockets of pristine habitat remain along floodplains of large rivers. The island is divided into West Java, Central Java, and East Java Provinces. Jakarta on the Java Sea was the Dutch colonial center when the Sunda Islands were the center of the spice trade. It is still the largest and most important city in West Java and in all of Indonesia. At

the eastern end of West Java is Cirebon, an important archaeological site of old palaces.

The only *Betta* species reported from Java to date is *B. picta*.

Bali

Bali is dominated by the 10,000 foot (3,048 m) Mount Agung and other volcanic mountains half its size. Lake Batur, a crater lake, sits atop Mount Batur at almost 4,000 feet (1,219 m). To the west are Lake Bratan, Lake Duyan, and Lake Tamblingan. The south of Bali has vast lowlands, but the many streams at different elevations offer many different habitats. The main rivers drain southward to the Indian Ocean or southeastward toward the Badung Strait separating Bali from Penida Island.

Bali is the last major island at the edge of the southeastern part of the

The island of Borneo hosts three nations: Brunei is independent, Sabah and Sarawak comprise eastern Malaysia, and Kalimantan is the westernmost part of Indonesia.

Sunda Shelf. The genus *Betta* has not yet been reported from Bali, but that may be the result of extensive development and loss of habitat. If contemplating a visit (and collecting) in Indonesia, Bali should not be an aquarist's first choice. Nor does the genus range across the deep strait separating this island from lands of the Sahil or Australian Shelf.

Borneo

Borneo is the largest and most exotic of the Sunda Islands. In the south, 75 percent of Borneo is the Indonesian state of Kalimantan. The northern portion of Borneo consists of the independent nation of Brunei, located between the Eastern Malaysia provinces of Sarawak and Sabah. At the northern tip of Borneo is Banggi Island across the South Banggi Strait, the smaller Balambangan Island immediately to the west, Jambongan Island along the southeastern coast, and Timbun Mata Island in the far southeast of the province. No large islands occur off the west coast.

Brunei

Brunei Darussalam, the Sultanate of Brunei, is a bifurcated nation in northwest Borneo. It faces the South China Sea and is surrounded by Sarawak. Eastern and western Brunei are separated by the deeply indenting Bay of Brunei. Bukit Pagon is the only large city in eastern Brunei at the border with Sarawak, and is drained by the Temborang River. Western Brunei is drained by the Wasah, Tutong, and Belait Rivers, and its major city is Bandar Seri Begawan. The only *Betta* reported from Brunei is *B. macrostoma,* the most beautiful species in the genus, and protected in Brunei.

Malaysia

The northern 80 percent of Borneo Island belongs to Malaysia except for the small enclave of Brunei. In the east and north, Borneo is occupied by the Malaysian Sabah Province. In the southwest of north Borneo, Sarawak Province (Malaysia) is the dominant political unit. The independent sultanate of Brunei occupies a coastal enclave in Sarawak.

Sabah is mountainous in the north and inland, with vast coastal plains in the east facing the Sulu Sea. A peninsula divides Sabah into north and south regions. Wildlife sanctuaries abound throughout Sabah.

Sarawak, at twice the size of Sabah, occupies most of northwestern Borneo. It faces the South China Sea. The mountains are entirely inland along its eastern border with Kalimantan (of Indonesia). The west coast is entirely lowlands, with alluvial plains along the rivers and extensive mangrove and freshwater swamps. The main cities are Sibu in the west and Kuching in the far west.

Betta species reported from Sabah or Sarawak in eastern Malaysia include *B. imbellis, B. macrostoma, B. ocellata, B. climacura, B. akarensis, B. balunga,* and *B. brownorum.*

Kalimantan

The southern two-thirds of Borneo is occupied by Kalimantan, the largest geographic region of Indonesia. Kalimantan is bordered by Sabah in the northeast, Sarawak in the north, the Java Sea in the south, and the Sulawesi Sea in the east. Sulawesi occurs across the Makassar Strait, a deepwater channel beyond the eastern end of the Sunda Shelf. The largest islands off Kalimantan are Maratua in the northeast, Laut in the southeast, and Karimata in the west. The 1:1,500,000 Nelles map of Kalimantan (Indonesia #4) includes coverage of Sabah, Sarawak, and Brunei.

Mining and timbering have degraded the interior, with the loss of primeval forests supporting orangutans and rare birds. These facilities require new roads into the interior, and scientists are making good use of them. New *Betta, Parosphromenus,* and other fishes are continually being discovered and reported in scientific journals, such as *Ichthyological Explorations in Freshwaters*, edited by Dr. Maurice Kottelat.

Kalimantan is divided into the four provinces of East Kalimantan, South Kalimantan, Central Kalimantan, and West Kalimantan.

At the capital of Pontianak on the west coast, the Landak River empties into a main tributary of the Kapuas, the greatest river basin in Borneo. The ancient Kapuas River dates back to the time of the largely extinct Sunda River, yet survives. The Kapuas provides transport upriver much of its 686 miles (1,104 km) length to inland cities and to its headwaters near Sarawak. The best reference on Kapuas River fishes is Roberts (1989), although several of the named fishes have subsequently been determined to be new species.

East Kalimantan itself is the eastern edge of the Sunda Shelf, and is the oldest part of this vast area in which *Betta* and its close relative *Parosphromenus* evolved. It has had a different history than the rest of Borneo, and its rivers and relationships of its fishes are not clear.

Betta species reported from Kalimantan include *B. albimarginata, B.*

Betta taeniata

anabatoides, B. breviobesus, B. channoides, B. dimidiata, B. edithae, B. enisae, B. foerschi (= strohi), B. patoti, B. pinguis, B. rutilans, and *B. unimaculata.* In my opinion, several of the "species" reported from Kalimantan, and previously reported from Sumatra and other Sunda islands, are not those species at all. Borneo has been isolated for more than 6,000 years, time enough for speciation. What looks similar to a Sumatran or Malay Peninsula species by this time is probably genetically and physiologically distinct. For this reason, it is incumbent upon aquarists to maintain geographic isolates separately, anticipating that many found will be new species. This already occurred with two species of *Parosphromenus* reported by Roberts from Borneo and later determined to be new species by Kottelat.

Chapter Eight
Betta Genetics

Some of the world's best breeders don't understand genetics. Mention the terms *back-cross, test-cross, dominant,* or *recessive,* and they roll their eyes. They rely on linebreeding.

The Basics

Linebreeding began when our ancestors in Africa planted seeds from wild grains, and saved seeds of the best plants for next year's planting. Every farmer, dog, cat, canary, and betta breeder uses linebreeding. Pick the best offspring and breed them to each other or their parents, then pick the best offspring again, and breed them to each other or their parents, and so on. You can pick breeding stock with different traits, such as richest color and fastest growth, and combine them in the offspring, and do this with disease resistance or anything else. Repeating the selection of the best of the young for new breeding stock enhances the traits the breeder wants to emphasize.

In 1859 Charles Darwin inadvertently made the connection between nature and linebreeding when he wrote that better and better adaptations of offspring to changing environments resulted in descendents different from their ancestors. He realized that gradual adaptation to a changing world was nature's linebreeding. Not everyone knew about Darwin's concept of evolution. Gregor Mendel didn't know.

Mendel cultivated peas that had pink, white, or red flowers. Like many other people, he linebred trying to get pure red or pure white strains. But unlike other people, Mendel kept records of his parental stocks and offspring colors. Soon he realized that the ratios of colors in his experiments were mathematically reproducible. Excited, he spoke at a meeting of scientists where he postulated the interactions of "factors" in garden peas that controlled flower color. At that fateful 1865 meeting, the science of genetics was born. Without knowing it, Mendel had provided both a proof and a mechanism for Darwin's new Theory of Evolution.

It would be 44 years before Mendel's factors would be renamed "genes."

By the early nineteenth century, chemists knew that proteins were made of molecules called amino acids, and the process took place in the cell's cytoplasm.

In 1909, Phoebus Leven isolated a sugar-phosphate-base complex from the cell nucleus he called deoxyribonucleic acid, or DNA. DNA contains chemical bases called adenine, thymine, cytosine, and guanine (abbreviated A, T, C, and G). In 1950, Erwin Chargaff noticed that the amount of A was always equal to the amount of T, and the ratio of C to G was also 1:1. Scientists suspected this might be the material of genes, but couldn't explain how it worked.

The explanation became crystal clear in 1953 when James Watson and Francis Crick, looking at an X-ray photograph of a DNA crystal prepared by a technician, realized the chemical consisted of two strands wrapped around each other in a double helix. The two strands of sugar-phosphate units on the outside wrapped around each another with inner units of T attracted to A, and C attracted to G. Watson and Crick could now see how DNA could unwind to make more DNA or to make RNA (more on that later). And how it all could work as a code for genes.

The genetic code is the arrangement of DNA's bases. Almost every series of three serial bases (A,T,T or, for example, G,C,T) codes for one of the amino acids (or a related purpose). The winding and unwinding explains DNA's ability to replicate itself, but how does that translate to proteins?

Enter ribonucleic acid or RNA. RNA was known to differ from DNA in a couple of ways. First, its sugar was ribose rather than deoxyribose, and instead of adenine (A) it had a new base called uracil (U). Oddly, there was little RNA in the nucleus, but lots in the cytoplasm (and that's where proteins were made).

When the two DNA strands unwind, each strand can serve as a mold (template) for a complementary strand. That's how chromosomes (and their genes) can double during mitosis or meiosis. But in addition to making more of itself, DNA can also be a template for RNA.

When DNA makes complementary RNA, it gives the RNA a mirror image of its arrangement of A,T,T, etc. In other words, it transfers the genetic code. This coded RNA then leaks out of the nucleus and into the cytoplasm. Here the RNA passes the coded information to another kind of RNA fixed inside microsomes (tiny organs along an intricate and invisible membrane inside the cytoplasm). Inside these microsomes, the RNA gathers individual amino acids *in the precise order* instructed by the nuclear DNA.

The sequence of amino acids in a continuous string follows the sequence of bases in the DNA (the code) that started this process. When the string of microsomal RNA

How the Code Works

We knew the genetic code was analogous to Morse code. But instead of two alternatives (dots and dashes) in 39 combinations for the letters of the English alphabet and Arabic numerals, there are four alternatives (adenine, thymine, cytosine, and guanine) in more than enough combinations for all the amino acids, the alphabet of proteins. In fact, we know today that of 64 possible triplet combinations of A, T, C, and G along a DNA strand, 61 code for one of the 20 amino acids (some triplets are redundant), and three triplets code for protein termination (start or stop points).

is filled with the specific amino amino acids (every triplet taken), the amino acids hook to each other and peel off, and then fold and hook some more into that single, specific, highly complex cluster of amino acids that we call a protein.

What does a gene look like? Pick any cell in the body and pluck out the nucleus. Then pluck out the chromosomes and uncoil all the strands of DNA. Stretched out, the DNA in a cell would be about five feet long. There are 30,000 to 100,000 genes in a human or a fish. These genes represent perhaps ten percent of the DNA, with the rest having other functions.

So does a gene code for an amino acid, a protein, or a trait?

What is a trait? A trait like flower color or color in bettas is controlled by one *or more* genes. The gene is a specific arrangement of some of the As, Ts, Gs, and Cs in a specific location on a specific chromosome, and it provides the code or instructions for making one particular protein. If a sequence of three bases (a triplet) of A, T, C, and G is the code for a particular amino acid, then that triplet is called a codon. One codon is the code for one amino acid. A strand of DNA contains many codons, but it also includes DNA areas that are inactive (we think). Because a protein consists of hundreds of amino acids, a gene is a long string of codons, perhaps a thousand of them, and separated by other codons that say "begin here" and "end here."

For the system to operate, there will be areas of DNA where amino acids are *not* made, so that the proteins are kept apart and cannot contaminate each other during synthesis.

So does a gene code for a trait or a protein? From the perspective of a scientist, a gene codes for a protein. From the perspective of a betta breeder, a gene codes for a trait, such as eye, fin, or body color, fin length, blood type, or growth rate. Some traits are controlled by one gene (one long segment of codons on one chromosome), and other traits appear when several genes work together. A betta breeder might consider blue color or elongate fin the result of a single gene, and he might be right, but it's more likely the trait is controlled by several genes. Some day we'll know, when we have a complete chemical analysis of betta DNA.

We've worked out the multiple codons (triplets) that code for many single genes and therefore specific proteins. But there is also a lot of DNA that doesn't seem to code for anything. We call it (erroneously) junk DNA. But it isn't junk at all.

Some triplets (codons) are redundant for the same amino acid. Other triplets code for stop, start, or operate as on or off switches along the DNA strand. There are also promoter regions in DNA. For example, proteins leaching from muscle fibers can enter the nucleus of muscle cells and attach to DNA to "promote" the coding for additional muscle fiber proteins. Proteins in other tissues do the same, instructing (promoting) the DNA to make tissue-specific proteins, such as the hormone insulin inside pancreas cells or sex hormones in gonad cells. Promoting is just one function of non-coding (junk) DNA.

So that's what a gene is and how it works. Every individual has many thousands of pairs of genes, one member of each pair from each parent. Some traits are controlled by one gene and others by a few genes. Some of what we see is controlled by many genes, traits such as fin length or shape, body color, or growth rate. Old-fashioned Mendelian genetics is useful for estimating how a gene works, or how a cluster of genes works when it behaves like just one because the genes are typically inherited together (linked). But few traits are the result of one gene.

Some traits are inherited in other ways. Not all DNA is in the nucleus. DNA is also found in mitochondria (where oxygen is used) and in chloroplasts and other plastids. The obvious conclusion is that these structures are remnants of ancient symbiotic microbes whose DNA was incorporated into modern cells as permanent parasites. Extra-nuclear DNA is inherited by subsequent generations, but there's a catch. Because the male provides only a sperm nucleus, whereas a female provides an egg nucleus plus a cytoplasm and mitochondria (and sometimes plastids in plants), the mitochondrial and plastid DNA is passed down only from females.

Mendel Revisited

We can assume there is one gene to a "trait" or that a trait is controlled by a series of linked genes that act like one gene. Although we don't know the complete DNA sequence of *Betta splendens*, we know some of the genes and gene clusters that control traits of color and finnage. How can we use this information?

We can use Mendelian genetics to predict interactions of genes (or gene clusters) that control fin shape, fin length, and body color in bettas, and so the percent (ratios) of each type of offspring based on the parental types. Often, however, the ratios of different types in the offspring do not match those predicted by Mendelian genetics, and new forms may appear in the offspring. Why?

Betta "genes" (as we know them) are probably *not* single sequences of codons. Each so-called gene may be several sequences on one or even different chromosomes working to produce a single outcome (phenotype). For example, we talk about five or so genes for color (red, yellow, nonred, black). Now we know that melanin (just one color) is a polymer of the amino acid phenylalanine and that black pigment results from different enzymes that eventually change phenylalanine into a polymer, hook it to a protein, and then oxidize the protein-polymer complex. Each enzyme in the series that converts phenylalanine to melanin is different. It is of course a protein (all enzymes are proteins) and so it must be coded by a different gene, and sometimes by more than one. So black pigment results from several genes producing several enzymes that work together. The same is probably true of red (and there are different proteins that can produce red or the lack of it), blue, yellow, or orange. There is probably no color in bettas produced by just a single enzyme.

Things Get Complicated!

Let's imagine each gene as perhaps thirty thousand A, T, G, and C bases making up 250 or more codons along a DNA chain. We also know that within a gene for a particular protein, there are coding segments (called exons) separated by noncoding sequences (called introns). Why? Probably to separate the amino acids so that they are made at just the right distances from one another to allow them to unpeel and collapse into just the right protein. In other words, the noncoding introns are "rails" or "fences" that keep production lines from running into each other. We've already mentioned codons whose only function is to turn genes on or off. So a *Betta* could be carrying genes for a trait, but we don't know because the genes were turned off by another gene. And finally, there are genes not just alongside other genes, but even within—yes, inside—other genes. Genes are more complicated than Gregor Mendel ever imagined. That's one reason Mendelian genetics doesn't always predict the results of a cross.

Alleles

Mendel showed that a gene can have more than one form. In the case of garden peas, Mendel opined that each parent provided a red flower gene or a white flower gene to any individual offspring. If the offspring inherited one of each gene from each parent, the flower was pink because the offspring inherited both kinds of gene and these genes interacted. If the offspring inherited two white genes, it would have only the one kind of allele and would produce white flowers. If it inherited two red genes, it would produce red flowers. The genes that could code for red or for white were later found to be in the identical position on the same chromosome. These two forms of the same gene are called alleles, because they code for alternative proteins (or conditions) along the same stretch of DNA.

The genetic difference between coding for red or white could be as simple as an alteration of a T or a G that results in a different amino acid, in turn resulting in a different protein with a different outcome. It's really simple if you consider that the alternative gene (allele) might result in a defective enzyme, eliminating a step in a series that leads to a usual outcome. In the case of albinos, yellows, browns, and blacks, it could be the inactivation of a single enzyme in the melanin pathway, so the black color never develops beyond one of the intermediary (and different color) stages.

We discuss bettas as though there were always two alleles for a trait. However, there may be a dozen or more alleles for that trait, but only two, three, or four common alleles. When we say common, we mean that they are the most common alleles in the population. For example, in a population of a million bettas, 90 percent may have three or four alleles for red color among them, whereas the remaining 10 percent have an additional 9 or 10 alleles affecting the same color

Amino Acids

Amino Acid	Abbreviation
Alanine	Ala
Arginine	Arg
Asparagine	Asn
Aspartic Acid	Asp
Cysteine	Cys
Glutamic Acid	Glu
Glutamine	Gln
Glycine	Gly
Histidine	His
Isoleucine	Ile
Leucine	Leu
Lysine	Lys
Methionine	Met
Phenylalanine	Phe
Proline	Pro
Serine	Ser
Threonine	Thr
Tryptophan	Trp
Tyrosine	Tyr
Valine	Val

scattered among them. That's why surprises can occur any time. Not every surprise is a new mutation. It might simply be the appearance of a previously undetected allele.

Mutations vs. Alleles

Mutations can happen several ways. During the formation of an egg or sperm cell, a parental chromosome breaks and reattaches in another position, so a linkage is lost and another linkage may result.

The magnificent **Betta splendens.**

Another and important way is that DNA makes an error when it replicates itself. Instead of a T, there may be an A in that location, or a C or a G. The result can be no effect at all, a change in a single amino acid that doesn't show up as an effect, or a change in a single amino acid where the difference can produce a life-saving enzyme or not have it, leading to certain death. We can make alleles in the laboratory,

Consequence of a SIngle Amino Acid Change

Progeria, a rare disease that causes premature aging, causes children to die of old age at around age 13. Progeria is caused by a base change mutation in the Lamin A gene on chromosome 1 that results in coding for a guanine instead of an adenine. (The Lamin-A gene is a medical hotspot for at least six other diseases.)

but most alleles are there just waiting to be discovered. They are mutations that happened long ago, and that did not keep that population from surviving. So with a tip of the hat to modern molecular genetics, let's look at the application of Mendelian Genetics to *Betta splendens*, and then try to explain what might be at work when our predictions don't go as planned.

DNA and RNA Triplet Codes

- A,A,A—phenylalanine (in nuclear RNA it is U,U,U)
- C,C,G—proline (in nuclear RNA it is G,G,C)
- C,C,A—glycine (in nuclear RNA it is G,G,T)

An opposite (matching) set is made by the formation of nuclear premessenger RNA from DNA. This premessenger RNA carries the information to the cytoplasm where it is edited (cut and pasted) into messenger (transfer) RNA. This is the RNA that takes amino acids and strings them into proteins.

(Methionine is not just for proteins, but is also used to initiate a sequence of codons after a gap [the intron]. The controller section of a gene is "upstream" of the main series of codons, and can activate or inactivate the DNA so it does or does not make the special RNA that makes a special protein for one kind of cell.)

Triplet Codes

DNA	RNA	Amino Acid	DNA	RNA	Amino Acid
AAG	UUC	phenylalanine	ATA	UAU	tyrosine
TAA	AUU	isoleucine	TTA	AAU	asparagine
AGA	UCU	serine	CTT	GAA	glutamic acid
TGA	ACU	threonine	TCA	AGU	serine
AAT	UUA	leucine	ATG	UAC	tyrosine
TAG	AUC	isoleucine	TTG	AAC	asparagine
AGG	UCC	serine	CTC	GAG	glutamic acid
TGG	ACC	threonine	TCG	AGC	serine
AAC	UUG	leucine	ATT	UAA	stop
TAT	AUA	isoleucine	TTT	AAA	lysine
AGT	UCA	serine	ACA	UGA	stop
TGT	ACA	threonine	TCT	AGA	argenine
GAA	CUU	leucine	ATC	UAG	stop
TAC	AUG	methionine	TTC	AAG	lysine
AGG	UCG	serine	ACC	UGG	tryptophan
TGC	ACG	threonine	TCC	AGG	argenine
GAG	CUC	leucine	GTA	CAU	histidine
CAA	GUU	valine	CTA	GAU	aspartic acid
GCA	CCU	proline	GCA	CGU	argenine
CGA	GCU	alanine	CCA	GGU	glycine
GAT	CUA	leucine	GTC	CAC	histidine
CAG	GUC	valine	CTG	GAC	aspartic acid
GGG	CCC	proline	GCG	CGC	arginine
CGG	GCC	alanine	CCG	GGC	glycine
AAA	UUU	phenylalanine	GTT	CAA	glutamine
CAT	GUA	valine	ACA	UGU	cysteine
GGT	CCA	proline	GCT	CGA	arginine
CGT	GCA	alanine	CCT	GGA	glycine
GAC	CUG	leucine	GTC	CAG	glutamine
CAC	GUG	valine	ACG	UGC	cysteine
GGC	CCG	proline	GCC	CGG	arginine
CGC	GCG	alanine	CCC	GGG	glycine

Chapter Nine

Breeding Bettas

It took two decades for French aquarists to learn that when male bettas blew bubbles, they were not suffocating but constructing a nest. When they figured that out, they became the first westerners to breed fighting fish.

Conditioning

Today's beginning aquarists typically find bettas easy to breed. It's a matter of knowing what to do and then doing it. The most reliable way to get them to breed is first to condition the adult male and female separately for two weeks. During this time you should feed them rich foods, especially live black worms, frozen bloodworms, or live brine shrimp from your pet store. If these foods are not available, you can use frozen meaty substitutes from the pet store, especially the rich frozen foods preferred by breeders of discus and marine fishes. Your dealer will know what's particularly nutritious and appropriate for bettas. You can also purchase supermarket seafoods and meats. Nutritious supermarket foods

suitable for bettas are chicken and beef liver, beef heart, any edible fish, shrimp, and oysters, but not clams (they are too tough). Frozen foods should be grated or blended into small particles that won't choke your fish, and then washed in a net with tap water to wash away juices that might pollute the water in which the adults are held. Conditioning takes about two weeks, and is complete when the male spends all his time working on a higher than normal bubblenest, and the female becomes wide with ripened roe and displays a white spot that resembles a ripe egg at her vent, or gonopore. The male never displays a white vent spot. (The white vent spot is a useful way to distinguish females from short-finned males.)

The Breeding Tank

Yes, it's true. Size matters. The usual breeding aquarium is a 5–10 gallon (20–40 L) tank, although tanks up to 50 gallon (200 L) are preferred because they are easier to keep clean. The additional water volume diletes the growth-inhibiting effects of nitrogenous wastes emitted by the fast-growing young. Diluting these wastes (using large tanks or frequent water changes) results in young fish growing more evenly than if crowded (in which case there are usually one or two large fish and all the rest are dwarfs). On a practical level, it's faster and less work to clean one 50 gallon (200 L) tank than to clean ten 5 gallon (20 L) tanks.

The tank is filled to a depth of 6 inches (15 cm) with new tap water, chemically dechlorinated. A floating thermometer is placed in the water, with a small heater (50 watts or less) added to maintain the temperature at 78°F (25°C). The water should be allowed to equilibrate with the room environment for two days. This allows enough time for any required thermostat adjustments, and for the supersaturated air in fresh tap water to come out of solution and dissipate into the atmosphere. If fish are placed in dechlorinated tap water too soon, air escaping from solution may attach to the fish's gills and oxidize (burn) the gill tissue.

The tank should also contain abundant plants. Plants provide a hiding place, or refuge, for a potentially attacked female and for slower-growing fry that need to escape their larger cannibalistic brethren. They also supply surface area for the growth of microscopic food upon which newborns depend and support for the nest. A dense clump of submerse plants, such as Java moss (*Vesicularia*), provides an ideal refuge. Floating plants, such as water sprite (*Ceratopteris*), provide surface structure to support the bubblenest. Other surface structures could be 4–6 inches (10–15 cm) diameter plastic food container lids, Styrofoam drink cups sliced in half lengthways, or pieces of Styrofoam. Many kinds of household or food containers, especially those made of translucent plastic, naturally float and are also suitable nesting sites for supporting a hidden bubblenest.

Do not aerate the tank. The release of air bubbles disrupts the surface film, interferes with the structural integrity of the bubblenest, and stimulates vibrations that cause the eggs to break free from the bubbles and sink. The upwelling currents will push the fry away from the oxygen-rich surface film. The tank should be largely covered to protect the water surface from evaporative chilling and to keep oils in airborne dust particles from producing an oily sheen that interferes with the diffusion of oxygen and carbon dioxide through the surface.

The First Date

Place the male in the tank first, and allow him time to take over that territory. Two days is a good period during which he can investigate the tank and then decide it belongs to him. His territoriality contributes to his decision to nest there, and a day later he will probably start building a bubblenest.

A female **Betta bung bihn.**

Two or three days after the male has been placed in the breeding tank, you can net the female from her conditioning aquarium and place her in a half-filled quart (1 L) jar. The reason the jar is half-filled is to make it float, no matter how much water is in the breeding tank, and to provide a wall over which neither fish can jump. With the jar floating in the breeding tank, the fish can see each other, but neither can jump into the other's space at this time.

By now the male has built a bubblenest, whether the female is in view or not. Once you have added the jar with the female, he gets excited (well, who wouldn't?) and vigorously adds bubbles to increase the height (more than the diameter) of his bubblenest. He seems torn between attending to his nest and attending to the female, constantly interrupting his bubble-blowing to charge toward her, biting and pushing the jar, undulating back and forth before her, fins spread grandly and gill covers flared.

The female may be unimpressed and, in that case, will ignore his antics. If this happens, leaving her there for a week won't make any difference. Set up a different match.

Usually, a well-conditioned female will be attentive to the male's efforts. She will respond by becoming darker and ramming the glass as though anxious to be with the male. Don't overrate this response. It may only mean she wants to play games with him, but isn't ready for a serious relationship. She is probably not ready for spawning until dark vertical bands appear on her flanks. These bands are pronounced in wild bettas; but, in Cambodians and other strains, these bands may be masked by a lack of melanin, a surface sheen of iridocytes, or dense red (pterin) pigmentation. So the absence of bands is not necessarily bad news. But neither is their presence a guarantee of imminent spawning. Hence, the importance of the dense vegetation as a refuge. She'll spawn when she's ready, and that might be a day or two later. This is also another reason why larger tanks are better; they give the female a better opportunity to escape.

The consequences of putting a male ready to spawn with a female not ready to spawn can be deadly for the female. Males of many fish species harass females with chasing, butts, and nips; but, male bettas bite and bite hard, often ripping the fins of females or opening wounds on their flanks. The result may be an infection that kills the female. Fighting fish are well named, and you should take the name seriously, always considering the welfare of a female who might not be physiologically prepared to spawn. Keep in mind that conditioning may help develop her eggs within the ovaries, but ripening of the eggs so they are receptive to fertilization may take some days, and behavior is not always reliable in determining when she is fertile and ready. Keep that back-up hiding place available. Even if you don't need it for this spawning, it will provide hiding places and a feeding station for the resulting babies.

After two or three days for the fish to become accustomed to one another, the female should be released into the tank with the male by tipping the jar. Watch both fish for at least a half hour to be certain she is not being damaged, although minor aggression is normal. If torn fins or wounds appear, the female should be immediately removed and retired for recovery, and another conditioned female selected for spawning.

Spawning

The male's first reaction to the released female is to circle her, displaying frantically, undulating so hard you might think he'd break his back, and then trying to lead her (by example) to the bubblenest. If the female is not ready, she'll refuse and head for cover or try to get out of the tank. If she is receptive, she'll eventually follow him to the nest. This foreplay could take an hour or a day before the first false spawnings. False, because the first few efforts to reach consummation are never successful. The fish need to adjust to each other.

The ritualized spawning act is as follows: The female meets the male beneath the nest, and he tries to wrap around her by bending his body into a U-shape around her body. This takes a while, as they try to fit comfortably together, she tilted perpendicular to him, and both their bodies angled so their vents are in close apposition. Once he succeeds in getting a firm grip on her, he squeezes his body hard around her, and it looks likes he's hugging her as hard as he can. Again, this will happen several times unsuccessfully, with them breaking apart with nothing coming of all the effort. Then, suddenly, they'll succeed. The squeeze will end with a violent trembling motion as both fish reach climax and he ejaculates milt, the female simultaneously releasing about a dozen small white eggs that tumble from their embrace.

Sometimes the female recovers first and goes after the sinking eggs (which she may eat or put in the nest), but more often the male recovers first. He makes a beeline for the eggs, picks them up in his mouth, and then goes to the nest, where he spits or shoots the eggs, together with a mouthful of bubbles, to the bottom of the nest. He may add another blast or two of air bubbles before he goes back to the female for another hug.

Male Betta splendens *guarding a nest.*

Spawning consists of many rounds of wrappings, climaxes, and releases of eggs, each lasting 15 minutes to an hour, and it can commence at any time of day. There may be a hundred or a thousand eggs in the total spawn. When the female is finished, having spent all her ripe eggs, she will try to leave, but the male will be insistent that he's not finished. That's another benefit of a refuge. If she didn't need it before, she certainly needs it now.

If you didn't see them spawning, you can still tell it has occurred. The female will have a different pattern, she will be hiding, and she may look thin and bedraggled, or even damaged. A close look beneath the bubblenest with a flashlight and a hand lens, or a pair of strong reading glasses (2.5×), will reveal the opaque white eggs tucked among the clear bubbles.

At this time, without disturbing the male and the bubblenest, remove the female to another tank and give her tender loving care (no tankmates, light feeding with nutritious and preferably live foods, heat about 80°F (29°C), and moderate aeration, siphoning the debris on the bottom daily), so she may fully recover.

Hatching

The bubblenest supports the eggs and early stage babies (prolarvae) not yet able to swim. Because the eggs and prolarvae are heavier than water, they would sink (in nature, into the muck at the bottom) if they could not attach to floating bubbles. The bubbles are coated with a sticky mucus to which the eggs will adhere. The eggs are stuck to the bubbles rather than enclosed within them.

Later the prolarvae themselves produce sticky mucus from head glands. This prolarval mucus assists in holding them at the oxygen-rich surface upon which they depend early in life before the labyrinth has been formed. This benefit is especially important to fishes that breed in stagnant, often polluted, water of low oxygen content. If there were nothing to hold them near the oxygen-rich surface film, they would perish in the lower reaches of the stagnant water.

At this early stage, the prolarvae are vulnerable to surface disturbances, and can be seen frequently dropping from the nest and darting up again in spirals, where they stick at least temporarily. Do not add any food, for it will only decay and foul the water. Prolarvae cannot feed, as they have no jaws, guts, useful eyes, or fins. They do not yet have functional gills and the labyrinth is well into the future. The prolarvae get all their nutrition from their yolk sacs and by absorption from the water, and they respire (absorb oxygen and release carbon dioxide) directly through their tissues. This stage lasts two or three days.

Feeding the Fry

At about the third day after hatching, the prolarvae become larvae (fry) with developed (black) eyes, jaws, functioning intestinal tracts, and fin buds now developing into fins. At this time, they can swim horizontally with control, search for food, and attack food. Their first food in nature consists of protozoa and other minute animals, such as rotifers, gastrotrichs, tiny worms, and the larvae of copepods and other crustaceans. In aquaria, we feed them cultured protozoa (you can purchase cultures and direc-

tions from many sources) or wild protozoa that you have grown from dried leaves, lettuce, or banana skins placed in a jar with water from a pond, outdoor container, or an established aquarium. The pond or tank water provides a seed stock of protozoans, and the plant material provides a culture medium upon which bacteria and fungi multiply. These bacteria and fungi are food for the seed stock of protozoans, which then multiply rapidly (bloom).

Sniff the jar. It should have a pleasant smell like hay on a farm field. Now hold the jar up toward the sky, and you will see the protozoa as a smoothly layered cloud of fine white particles. If you see only a gray cloud with wisps, no discrete white spots, and the jar smells bad, then you have grown only bacteria rather than protozoa, the culture has failed, and you need to throw it out and start over.

Alternative first foods are the dust at the bottom of packages of dried food, commercial liquefied fry preparations based on yeast and egg yolk, and even crumbled dried leaves from hardwood trees, such as sycamores, oaks, hickories, and maples. Just like the lettuce or banana skin method, these dried leaves, left in tank water for about a week, will develop a microscopic faunal community that provides an excellent and diverse food source. In this case, the protozoa are attached to, or glide along, the surfaces of the leaf bits.

Protozoa as whole culture water should be fed to the fry as soon as they swim horizontally. Feed the fry a cupful per 5 gallons (20 L) twice a day for three days. Feeding fry will develop plump opaque white bellies.

Two days into this regimen, begin feeding small quantities of live *Artemia* nauplii (baby brine shrimp). By day four or five of free-swimming, you can stop adding protozoa and feed brine shrimp nauplii (with or without microworms) exclusively. When the fry are feeding on baby brine shrimp, their bellies become salmon pink. (All these food growing and feeding procedures are explained further in Chapter 5.)

Grow-out

You will never raise an entire spawn of up to a thousand fry. You will raise a fraction, more in larger tanks, and relatively few (only 10–20 fish) in a small (5 gallon [20 L]) tank. In a small tank, you need only siphon out old water before replacing it with new (dechlorinated) water to make up for evaporation. If you are using a larger (20–50 gallon [80–200 L]) tank, then slowly increase the volume and water level by 1 inch (2.5 cm) each week. And at least weekly, preferably more often, siphon debris from the bottom while removing 10 to 25 percent of the old tank water, replacing this volume with dechlorinated, temperature-equilibrated, and degassed, tap water.

The best growth doesn't result from heavy or frequent feeding, or even the most nutritious foods, although they all help. Optimal growth (fast and even) is attained by frequent, massive water changes that remove the growth-inhibiting nitrogenous wastes of the fishes themselves. The expert angelfish breeder Dr. Joanne Norton changes 90 percent of the water daily. That's an extreme example, but her fish grow at extraordinarily rapid rates.

Culling

Culling is the hardest part of breeding bettas. Nobody likes it, but it's necessary to produce good quality fish from generation to generation. In culling, we remove and eliminate the slowest growing and deformed young. Many breeders feed these culled fish to larger predators. The objective is to save the fastest growing, best formed, and most colorful and best-finned fishes for two reasons. They have commercial or show value, and they are the future breeding stock of the next generation.

Unless you are a show or commercial breeder, culling is not necessary. There is no rule that you must remove or destroy baby fishes that don't measure up to some standard. If you want to keep all the fry, then keep them. Like people, the joy they experience from life and the joy they bring to you will have nothing to do with somebody's invented standards.

Chapter Ten
Other Anabantoids

A recent classification of anabantoids (Britz, 2001) sorts the genera into the following families and subfamilies based on head and jaw structure, egg features, and other structures:

Family Helostomatidae
       Genus *Helostoma*
Family Osphronemidae
    Subfamily Osphroneminae
       Genus *Osphronemus*
    Subfamily Belontiinae
       Genus *Belontia*
       Genus *Sandelia*
Family Anabantidae
       Genus *Anabas*
       Genus *Ctenopoma*
       Genus *Microctenopoma*
    Subfamily Luciocephalinae
       Genus *Luciocephalus*
       Genus *Trichogaster*
       Genus *Colisa*
       Genus *Ctenops*
       Genus *Parasphaerichthys*
       Genus *Sphaerichthys*
    Subfamily Macropodinae
       Genus *Betta*
       Genus *Macropodus*
       Genus *Pseudosphronemus*
       Genus *Parosphronemus*
       Genus *Trichopsis*
       Genus *Malpulutta*

Family Helostomatidae

Helostoma contains *H. temminkii*, the kissing gourami. This pink (sometimes green) planktivorous and herbivorous anabantoid feeds heavily on dried foods but prefers algae, and scatters thousands of floating eggs if housed and well-fed in a large aquarium. Sexes are similar.

Family Osphronemidae

Osphronemus contains the widely transplanted giant gouramy (*Osphronemus goramy*), endemic to the Mekong River drainage of southeast Asia, and two species from northern Borneo, *O. laticlavius* and *O. septemfasciatus*. *O. goramy* has also been called *O. satyrus, O. olfax,* and *O. notatus*. It is gray-brown with 8–10 diffuse vertical bands in the juvenile. *O. septemfasciatus* has dark-edged scales above the lateral line and red-edged scales below the lateral line, providing an illusion of dark and red horizontal stripes. *O. laticlavius* has a large black prepeduncular and subpeduncular spot and reddish unpaired fins in the juvenile and male, and a black spot at the base of the pectoral fin and a dark body with blackish unpaired fins in the male. Either sex of all species may have a nuchal hump (Roberts, 1992).

Belontia contains *B. hasselti* from the Sunda Shelf locales of Malaysia and Indonesia, and *B. signata* from Sri Lanka (Ceylon). Suitable for larger aquaria, these peaceful, attractive fishes are seldom imported.

Sandelia contains *S. capensis* and *S. bainesi* of southern South Africa. These large carnivores deposit adhesive eggs on the bottom. They have limited distributions and a need for clear, cold streams, and are presently threatened by habitat degradation. They are not available to aquarists.

Family Anabantidae

Anabas testudineus and *A. oligolepis*, the climbing perches, are widely distributed throughout Asia, mostly through transplantation into rice ponds for production of food fish, and even brackish water. They are omnivores that will even eat rice. Well-developed labyrinths allow them to survive for days in damp soil or vegetation. The thousands of floating eggs are unprotected.

Ctenopoma and *Microctenopoma* occur in different river basins of tropical Africa. About 2 dozen species of these "bushfish" are known, some that build weak bubblenests and provide care, and others that provide no bubblenest and no care. The nominal species include *C. acutirostre, M. ansorgei, M. argentoventer, M. congicum, M. damasi, M. fasciolatum, M. intermedium, C. kingsleyi, C. maculatum, M. milleri, C. multispinis, C. murel, M. nanum, M. nigricans, C. nigropannosum, C. ocellatum, M. ocellifer, C. oxyrhynchum, C. pellegrini, C. petherici, M. uelense,* and *M. weeksii.* All bushfish should have large (at least 20 gallon [76 L]) aquaria, with dense vegetation, and a rich insectivorous diet. Spawns are usually unexpected, but they range from a hundred to even thousands of eggs.

Luciocephalus pulcher, the pike head, is a widely distributed, elongate predator from Malaysia and Indonesia, and introduced throughout the Indo-Pacific. The wide distribution and variation in coloration suggest that it may be more than one species.

Trichogaster contains the best-known gouramies, the blue or three spot *(trichopterus),* pearl *(leeri),* moonlight *(microlepis),* and snakeskin *(pectoralis).* These peaceful insectivores thrive on dry food, and readily build a substantial bubblenest among floating plants. The blue gourami is produced in albino, xanthic, and brown variants, with or without spots, and with oblique bands (cosby gourami).

Colisa are stubby gouramies from separate river basins of India and

Burma (Myanmar). The four natural species are the dwarf (*lalia*), honey (*chuna*), banded (*fasciata*), and thick lipped (*labiosa*). The commercial market is now dominated by metallic and sunset variants, and hybrids of *lalia-chuna* and of *labiosa-fasciata*. They are not difficult to breed.

Ctenops nobilis occurs in stagnant, lowland streams of the Ganges and Brahmaputra drainages of India and Bangladesh. It resembles a sickly, thin, chocolate gourami, and never seems vigorous. Seldom imported, it is not popular.

Parasphaerichthys includes *P. ocellatus* from northern Burma (Myanmar) and the newly discovered *P. lineatus* from southern Burma (Britz and Kottelat, 2002). The former has a spot on the caudal peduncle and a larger midbody spot, whereas the new species has a dark, broken horizontal stripe on the flank. These minute bubblenesters are among the smallest of all anabantoids.

Sphaerichthys contains *S. osphromenoides*, the chocolate gourami, *S. vaillanti*, Vaillant's chocolate gourami, and *S. acrostoma*, the large chocolate gourami. A subspecies of *S. osphromenoides, S. o. selatanensis*, has reddish dorsal and anal fins. *S. vaillanti* has orange on the ventrum, the flanks, and the unpaired fins, and distinctive white margins and a horizontal band.

Macropodus contains *M. opercularis, M. ocellatus, M. spechti* (*M. concolor* is a synonym), *M. hongkongensis,* and *M. erythropterus* (Freyhof and Herder, 2002). *M. oper-*cularis is the common paradise fish, available in wild type, red, blue, and metallic strains. *M. ocellatus* is the round tailed paradise fish, available as an albino with orange bands, but the rarely imported wild type has an attractive dark color and pattern. *M. spechti* was previously known as the black paradise fish or *M. concolor*. *M. erythropterus* is almost identical, and both are from Vietnam, casting doubt on the validity of *M. erythropterus* in my opinion. *M. hongkongensis* is a muddy gray fish with a blue opercular spot.

Pseudosphronemus contains two rather drab species, *P. dayi* the spike tail and *P. cupanus* the redeye spike tail. Peaceful, they readily spawn in caves or beneath floating leaves, and the 50–150 fry are easily raised but are difficult to give away.

Parosphronemus is also spelled as *Parosphromenus* in aquarium literature, and I follow Kottelat in this book. This genus includes the licorice gouramies, with new species constantly being discovered throughout the Sunda Islands from the Malay Peninsula to Borneo. A partial list of species includes *P. allani, P. anjunganensis, P. deissneri, P. filamentosus, P. harveyi, P. linkei, P. nagyi, P. ornaticauda, P. paludicola,* and *P. parvulus*. In addition, populations representing several new species are reported as *P. sp.* from throughout Indonesia and Malaysia. The final number of species in this genus will be second only to those in *Betta*. They all require small shallow water tanks with little or no aeration, acidic, peat-stained, almost

Male fancy **Betta splendens.**

zero hardness water, shade, live foods, and caves for spawning. Some pairs are ready spawners, and success is more dependent on the pair than on the species.

Trichopsis are the croaking gouramies *T. vittata, T. schalleri,* and *T. pumilus*. All are small, easily spawned fishes with red, purple, and blue speckling in the fins, and two or more dark horizontal lines on the flanks. Spade-shaped caudal fins occur in either sex, but may be age related. Males have longer anal fins and may be larger than females. The

croaking noise can be heard with the unaided ear and is a characteristic of the genus.

Malpulutta contains *M. kretseri*, endemic to Sri Lanka (Ceylon), an island off the coast of India. The male is darkly beautiful, with long pointed and flowing unpaired fins, including an extended and almost arrow-like caudal fin. The predominant colors (in good males) are charcoal black and midnight blue, but stressed, immature, and female fish tend to plain dark gray. Not difficult to spawn, but seldom imported.

Glossary

ALLELE. A variant of a single gene, inherited at a particular genetic locus. One of two or more alternative forms of a gene, distinguishable from other forms or alleles of the same gene. For example, a species of flowering plant contains two alleles a_1 and a_2 which control the color of the seed coats; a single recessive gene controls the trait of albinism with two alleles a (albino) and A (normal). Two alleles on one locus produce three diploid genotypes: *AA, Aa, aa*. Addition of a second locus with two alleles B and b makes nine genotypes possible (*AABB, AABb, AaBB*, ...). In general, where each locus contains just two alleles, the number of possible genotypes in a population containing n of the loci is 3^n. In fact the number of alleles is usually higher, and so the general case is: the total number of genotypes that can be put together from all the n genotypes is $m_1 \times m_2 \times m_3 \times ... \times m_n$, where m_1 is the number of genotypes possible at the first locus, m_2 at the second, and so on. In humans, at least 10,000 loci exist, many of which carry numerous alleles. So the total number of diploid genotypes is astronomical. The commonness of an allele in a population is termed the "allele frequency."

ALLOZYME. Variant form of an enzyme (protein) that results from the presence of different alleles for the gene that produces the enzyme.

APOMORPH. Evolutionarily advanced (derived) character state. For example the long neck of the giraffe is apomorphic, the shorter neck of its ancestor is plesiomorphic.

AUTOSOME. Any chromosome in the cell nucleus other than a SEX CHROMOSOME.

BACK CROSS. A cross-fertilization made to identify hidden recessive alleles. An organism possessing a dominant characteristic can be shown to be homozygous for the character or heterozygous, by crossing it with one containing the recessive characteristic. If all the offspring have the dominant characteristic, then it is homozygous; if only half have it, then it is heterozygous.

CHROMATIN. The complex of DNA and proteins that makes up a eukaryotic chromosome.

CHROMOSOME. Complex structure found in the nucleus of a eucaryotic cell, composed of nucleic acids and proteins, and bearing part of the genetic information (genes) of the cell. Humans have 46 chromosomes (analogy: 46 filing cabinet drawers each containing pages, the genes, of DNA code, A-C-G-T..., written on them). The chromosomes are usually present in all cells in the body, even though only a minority of them will be active in any one cell.

CLADISTICS (PHYLOGENETIC SYSTEMATICS). A systematic method whereby taxa are hierarchically clustered according to inferred relative recency of common ancestry, based on their shared derived character states. It is based on the assumption that two new species are formed suddenly, by splitting from a common ancestor, and not by gradual evolutionary change. It has been used to argue that the major branching patterns of cladograms correspond to large-scale evolutionary events that cannot be explained by orthodox neo-Darwinism.

CLINE. Continuous gradation of form or gene differences in a population of a species, correlated with its geographical or ecological distribution. Clines usually take one of two forms: North/South, for example the spotting pattern of the Large Heath butterfly (*Coenonympha tullia*) in the British Isles; or altitudinal, for example the spotting pattern of the Corsican Heath butterfly (*Coenonympha corinna*) in Corsica.

CROSSING OVER. The reciprocal exchange of portions of chromatids between homologous chromosomes during meiosis. Crossing over produces recombination by altering the patterns of genes in a chromosome.

CYTOPLASMIC INHERITANCE. Non-Mendelian (extra-chromosomal) inheritance via genes in cytoplasmic organelles. Examples of such organelles are viruses, mitochondria, and plastids (e.g., chloroplasts). These all have their own genetic material, which is open to mutations that do not follow Mendel's rules for chromosomal genes. Although both male and female parents contribute equally to the zygote in terms of chromosomal genes, it is usually only the female parent that contributes the initial cytoplasm and organelles of the zygote. Zygotic development therefore usually begins within a maternal milieu, so maternal cytoplasm directly affects zygotic development. (See also SEX.)

DIPLOID Having two sets of genes and two sets of chromosomes, one from the mother and one from the father.

DNA (DEOXYRIBONUCLEIC ACID). The fundamental hereditary material of all living organisms. DNA is composed of a double-stranded helix of sugar phosphate held together by pairs of nucleotide bases in linear sequence. These nitrogenous bases are thymine, cytosine, guanine, and adenine (C-T-G-A), and the four bases in the two strands are always paired in such a way that A lies opposite T and G lies opposite C. DNA embodies the genetic code. Because of the complementary base-pairing the two strands of DNA can serve as original and template for the production of a new complementary partner strand. DNA therefore carries information by means of the linear sequence of its nucleotides, each of which can be considered as a letter in a simple four-letter alphabet that is used to write out biological messages in a linear "ticker-tape" form. Because the number of different possible sequences of a DNA chain that is n nucleotides long is 4^n, the amount of biological variety that can be generated using even a modest length of DNA is enormous. A single human cell comprises 1.5 m of DNA (5×10^9 nucleotide base pairs), organized into the 46 chromosomes that carry our genes. A single gene comprises about 1,000 base pairs.

EPISTATIC EFFECT. The production in an organism of a character determined by genes at two or more loci, different from the characters coded individually at each locus.

FISSION (allopatric speciation by). The intrusion of a new barrier divides a species into two isolated populations which then evolve into two species. If the barrier then disappears, the two new daughter species can coexist in the same habitat without interbreeding.

FIXATION. In population genetics, the complete prevalence of one gene form (allele), resulting in the complete exclusion of another.

FOUNDER EFFECT. When a new population is derived from a few immigrants, these founders represent a very small sample of the genetic pool to which they formally belonged; natural selection operating on this restricted variety soon yields gene combinations quite different from those found in the ancestral population, or those of a second small sample of founders.

GENE. A hypothetical unit of heredity. Genes are arranged in linear fashion on the chromosome, and each segregates as a single unit during meiosis and gives rise to a definable phenotypic trait. The "gene for blue eyes" is not one stretch of DNA solely responsible for causing eyes to be a particular color, but several sections of DNA-making enzymes that control various steps of the chemical reactions by which a pigment is synthesized or not. The genes that produce wrinkled seeds in peas comprise the strands of DNA that make the enzymes that critically affect the seed-wall building process, leading to partial loss of moisture and wrinkling. In most cases, a gene corresponds to a region of the genome that directs the synthesis of a single enzyme, so one gene corresponds with one polypeptide chain.

GENE POOL. All of the hereditary material (genes) in a population.

GENETIC CODE. The set of correspondences between base (nucleotide pair) triplets in DNA and amino acids in protein. These base triplets carry the genetic information for protein synthesis. For example, the triplet C-A-A codes for valine, 1 of the 20 amino acids found in proteins.

GENETIC DRIFT. The alteration of gene frequencies (evolution) through chance processes alone. For example if an *Aa* individual of *Drosophila* is crossed with another *Aa*, the offspring may not yield the exact 1:2:1 Mendelian ratio. If four individuals were selected *at random* from the offspring to start a new population, chance dictates that other ratios would obtain some of the time, and an allele could be lost entirely or fixed in a single step. Genetic drift is most likely to be effective in very small populations (<100 individuals), where reduction of genetic variability lowers the capacity of a population to adapt to changes in the environment, and also tends to reduce the overall fitness of the population. INBREEDING DEPRESSION expresses the same effect as small population size in promoting genetic drift, and genetic drift can also operate through the FOUNDER EFFECT: New populations start from a small number of pioneers, which contained only a small fraction of the alleles found in the source population, and so the new population differs at the beginning from its source.

GENETIC LOAD. The relative decrease in the mean fitness of a population as a result of the presence of genotypes that have less than the highest fitness. Genetic load is also the average number of lethal mutations per individual in a population.

GENETIC MARKERS. Molecular methods for making inferences about descent. These include allozymes, restriction fragment length polymorphisms (RFLPs), multilocus minisatellite or DNA fingerprints, single locus minisatellites or variable number of tandem repeats (VNTRs), randomly amplified polymorphic DNA (RAPDs), microsatellites, and mitochondrial DNA (mtDNA). Among the newer methods, minisatellites can provide a similarity index for populations, microsatellites reveal information about kinship, and mitochondrial DNA determines the maternal contribution to descent. [See Queller, D.C. *et al.* 1993. *TREE*, 8:285.]

GENOME. The complete genetic constitution of a eukaryotic organism. The full genome of an individual is borne by a single representative of each of all the chromosome pairs in a nucleus. The human genome consists of 3 billion base pairs of DNA, encoding approximately 30,000 genes (the functions of which are unknown for the vast majority). All the genes contained in a single set of chromosomes (i.e., in a haploid nucleus).

GENOTYPE. An exact description of the genetic constitution of an individual, with respect to a single trait or set of traits. PHENOTYPE is the product of the genotype interacting with the environment. Some expressions of the genotype are resistant to the effects of the environment (blood type, eye color), others are more readily influenced (stature, athleticism).

HAPLOID. Having a chromosome complement consisting of just one copy of each chromosome; c.f. DIPLOID, consisting of two copies (homologues) of each chromosome. A diploid individual usually arises as a result of the fusion of two haploid GAMETES (egg and sperm). Thus the two homologues in each chromosome pair in a diploid cell are of separate origin, one derived from the female parent and one from the male. In diploid organisms, only the gametes are haploid.

HETEROZYGOUS. Of a diploid organism having different alleles of a given gene on the pair of homologues carrying that gene. Because a heterozygote has two or more different alleles at a given locus, it does not breed true. Presence of different alleles at a particular gene locus.

HOMOLOGUE. One of a pair, or larger set, of chromosomes having the same overall genetic composition and sequence. In diploid organisms, each chromosome inherited from one parent is matched by an identical (except for mutational changes) chromosome—its homologue—from the other parent.

HOMOZYGOUS. Of a diploid organism having identical alleles of a given gene on both homologous chromosomes. An organism may be a homozygote with respect to one gene and, at the same time, a heterozygote with respect to another.

HYBRID. The offspring of a mating in which the parents belong to different varieties or species. Hybrid species are often sterile, but may show increased vigor (heterosis), in terms of strength, disease resistance, life span, and so on.

HYBRID VIGOR (HETEROSIS). The increase in size or rate of growth or fertility or survival (e.g., resistance to disease) associated with increased heterozygosity. It usually results from crosses between two genetically different, highly inbred lines.

INBREEDING DEPRESSION. A loss of vigor among offspring occurring when closely related individuals mate, resulting from the expression of numbers of deleterious genes in a homozygous state and from a generally low level of heterozygosity.

INTRONS. Stretches of DNA sequences that divide the coding sequence of a gene into two or more parts termed exons. After the gene is transcribed into RNA, intron sequences are spliced out of the RNA sequence, a process called RNA splicing. First discovered in 1977, introns have been found in numerous eukaryote nuclear and organelle (chloroplasts and mitochondria) genes. Introns can be amplified by PCR, and they appear to have a similar rate of evolution to the gene, and higher than that of the axon (which is very conserved). Introns are, therefore, potentially of interest as GENETIC MARKERS. The base pair sequence differences should provide information directly about the rate of evolution, rather than producing banding patterns as in microsatellites and allozymes. [See Liu, X. 1991. *BioEssays*, 13:185.]

ISOZYME (ISOENZYME). Different molecular forms of what is functionally the same enzyme. If two or more isozymes are coded for by different alleles at the same locus they are allozymes.

KARYOTYPE. The number and structure of the chromosomes in the nucleus of a cell. All the diploid cells of an organism have identical karyotype.

LETHAL-EQUIVALENT ALLELES. Alleles whose summed effect is that of lethality. For example, four alleles, each of which would be lethal 25 percent of the time (or to 25 percent of their bearers), are equivalent to one lethal allele. The average human carries about four lethal-equivalent alleles that are hidden as recessive alleles (estimated from inbreeding data).

LINKAGE. The presence on the same chromosome of two or more loci, usually recognized by the statistical tendency for alleles at linked loci to be inherited together. For example, if hair and eye color are linked, offspring that inherit their mother's eye color will also inherit her hair color.

LOCUS. The position of a gene in a chromosome. If the gene has several alleles (i.e., takes several forms), only one of these will be present at a given locus.

MEIOSIS. Cell division of a diploid cell to produce four haploid daughter cells. The process consists of two successive cell divisions with only one cycle of chromosome replication. It is a tenet of population genetics that meiotic segregation occurs independently of the fitness of the resulting zygote [but see Pomiankowski, A. & Hurst, L.D. 1993. *Nature*, 363:6428]. Moreover, the gametes produced after normal meiosis have a 50 percent probability of containing a given member of a pair of homologous chromosomes (the random assortment of chromosomes prescribed by traditional Mendelian genetics). However, some instances occur where the segregation of chromosomes at meiosis is not fair and one of a particular pair of homologues is inherited more frequently than the other. This is described as MEIOTIC DRIVE.

MENDELIAN INHERITANCE. Non-blending inheritance by means of pairs of discrete hereditary factors (now identified with genes), one member of each pair coming from each parent. The main theoretical alternative is blending inheritance. In Mendelian inheritance genes may blend in their effects on a body, but they themselves do not blend, and they are passed on intact to future generations. (See also CYTOPLASMIC INHERITANCE.)

MICROSATELLITE MARKERS. Segments of DNA with tandem repeats of short-sequence motifs. They are numerous, highly variable and easy to score using the POLYMERASE CHAIN REACTION, making them excellent genetic markers for kinship studies. For example, a sequence for a wasp has a microsatellite consisting of ten A-A-T repeats. Other alleles at this locus have different numbers of repeats. When DNA at the microsatellite locus is amplified using PCR techniques and then electrophoresed through a gel to separate the alleles, each allele shows a characteristic three-band pattern. Alleles with fewer A-A-T repeats are smaller and migrate further down the gel. Microsatellites are unusual in that they mutate relatively frequently, generating new alleles that are thought to have little or no effect on an animal's fitness; if the members of a species mix and interbreed freely, then any new form of microsatellite will tend to spread homogeneously through the population. PCR primers can thus iden-

tify DNA motifs that evolve sufficiently rapidly to provide markers to characterize discrete populations. Character states are based on allele length and, therefore, are not irreversible: Individuals sharing alleles of the same length may do so by either relatedness or chance convergence (the mutation rate is estimated at 10^{-3} in mammals, so two populations more than a thousand generations apart cannot reliably be compared). An ideal system would be one in which new alleles are generated relatively frequently, but where the chances of back mutation are negligible (the infinite alleles model in which no alleles get mutated to twice). Minisatellite variable repeat (MVR) mapping may be a solution. Like DNA fingerprinting, this approach is based on minisatellites, but it maps the internal structure of a single locus (rather than measuring variations in length at one or several loci). [See Queller, D.C. *et al.* 1993. *TREE*, 8:285; Ashley, M.V. & Dow, B.D. 1994. In: *Molecular Ecology and Evolution: Approaches and Applications.* Berkhauser & Verlag, p:185; Wright, J.M. & Bentzen, P. 1994. *Rev. Fish Biol. Fisheries*, 4:384.]

MITOCHONDRIA. Semiautonomous organelles containing their own DNA and ribosomes and reproducing by binary fission, occurring in large numbers in the cytoplasm of eukaryotic cells. They are the major site of ATP production and, hence, oxygen consumption in cells.

MITOSIS. Cell division leading to the formation of two daughter cells each with a chromosome complement identical to that of the original cell.

MOLECULAR EVOLUTION. Substitution of one amino acid for another in protein synthesis as a result of mutation of the genetic code. According to the NEUTRALITY THEORY OF MOLECULAR EVOLUTION, the variability at the molecular level that results from mutation is caused by random drift of the mutant genes rather than by selection.

MUTATION. Mutations are either *point mutations*, molecular substitutions of some nucleotide pairs for others in the DNA molecule, or *chromosome aberrations*, major structural changes encompassing hundreds or thousands of nucleotide pairs. A change in the sequence of DNA base pairs resulting from substitution, addition, deletion, or rearrangement of the standard base pairs. Mutations do not damage the regularity of the genetic material, but they cause change of a character into another character.

NATURAL SELECTION. The differential contribution of offspring to the next generation by individuals of different genetic types but belonging to the same population. This is the basic mechanism of evolution proposed by Charles Darwin and is generally regarded today as the main guiding force in evolution. It predicts reproduction of the fittest, rather than survival of the fittest. It is the only one of the agents of evolution that specifically adapts populations to their immediate environment. In many animals it operates principally through differences in the reproductive success of individuals. Its result is always the same: Some genotypes gain in the population at the expense of others. The selective force can act on the variability of a population in three different ways: A normal distribution of the population, which arises from many factors contributing jointly and independently to the trait under consideration, say size, can have both tails pulled in by *stabilizing selection*, or one tail by *directional selection*, or be divided into two by *disruptive selection*. Natural selection is usually of overriding importance in MICROEVOLUTION.

OOGENESIS. Oogonia cells within the ovary divide mitotically to produce many oocytes. When mature, these undergo meiotic divisions to halve the number of chromosomes. The first produces a polar body and a secondary oocyte, and division of the latter produces an ovum and a second polar body.

OUTCROSSING. Mixing of genetic material from one individual with that from another.

PHENOTYPE. The observable manifestation of a specific genotype; the observable properties produced by the genotype in conjunction with its environment.

PHYLOGENY. The evolutionary relationships within and between taxonomic levels, particularly the patterns of lines of descent, often branching, from one species to another.

PLEIOTROPIC. A gene that affects more than one characteristic in the PHENOTYPE.

PLESIOMORPH. Primitive character state. (See also APOMORPH.)

POLYMORPHISM is the coexistence in the same population of two or more distinct hereditary types based on different alleles. The existence of two or more genetically distinct forms contained within the same breeding population.

POLYPHYLETIC. A group of species classified together is polyphyletic when some of its members have had quite distinct evolutionary histories, not being descended from a common ancestor that was also a member of the group; so, if the classification is to correspond with phylogeny, the group should be broken up into two or more distinct groups.

RECOMBINATION. During gamete formation, the phase of meiosis in which chromosomes cross over and DNA is exchanged between the pair. Recombination shuffles the combinations of genes linked on the same chromosome. Thus genes from different chromosomes can become linked, and linked genes on the same chromosome can become unlinked, as a result of recombination. The rearrangement of genes produces offspring that have a combination of characteristics different from that of their parents. Recombination is a random process.

RECOMBINANT DNA TECHNOLOGY (GENETIC ENGINEERING). Manipulation of DNA using restriction enzymes, which can split the DNA molecule and then join vector with foreign DNA to form a hybrid molecule of nonhomologous DNA called recombinant DNA. This technique bypasses all the biological restraints to genetic exchange and mixing, and even permits the combination of genes from widely different species.

RIBOSOMES. Granules composed of RNA and protein found in large numbers in all types of cells, where they synthesize protein.

RNA (RIBONUCLEIC ACID). Nucleic acid characterized by the presence of D-ribose and the pyrimidine base uracil. It occurs in three principal forms, as messenger-RNA, ribosomal-RNA, and transfer-RNA, all of which participate in protein synthesis.

RNA is ribonucleic acid, a close cousin of deoxyribonucleic acid, or DNA. RNA is a polymer of ribonucleoside-phosphates. Its backbone is composed of alternating ribose and phosphate groups. Ribose is a five-carbon sugar that is found in a puranose, or five-membered ring, form in RNA. The phosphate groups link consecutive ribose groups and each bear one negative charge. Each monomer also has a nitrogenous base for a side chain. The four commonly found side chains in RNA are adenine, cytosine, guanine, and uracil. Several other bases are occasionally found in RNAs including: thymine, pseudouridine, and methylated cytosine and guanine. Inside of cells, there are three major types of RNA: messenger RNA (mRNA), transfer RNA (tRNA), and ribosomal RNA (rRNA). There are a number of other types of RNA present in smaller quantities as well, including small nuclear RNA (snRNA), small nucleolar RNA (snoRNA) and the 4.5S signal recognition particle (SRP) RNA. Novel species of RNA continue to be identified.

SEX CHROMOSOME. In organisms with a chromosomal mechanism of sex determination, one of the chromosomes involved in sex determination. One sex chromosome, the X-chromosome, is present in two copies in one sex and only one copy in the other sex. The autosomes, as opposed to the sex chromosomes, are present in two copies in both sexes. In many organisms, there is a second sex chromosome, the Y-chromosome, that is found in only one sex—the sex having only one copy of the X. Sex-linked genes are those carried on the sex chromosomes.

SEXUAL REPRODUCTION. Reproduction involving the fusion of haploid nuclei, usually gametes, which result from MEIOSIS. Sexual reproduction creates diversity but does not force changes in gene frequencies. It is therefore the agent of adaptability but not of evolution. The population uses sexual reproduction to increase the diversity it needs to evolve, but sexual reproduction alone does not cause the population to evolve. Instead, the essential changes in gene frequencies are caused by four evolutionary agents: MUTATION PRESSURE, GENETIC DRIFT, GENE FLOW, and NATURAL SELECTION.

SPECIATION can result from two different mechanisms: allopatric (geographic) speciation, by simple FISSION or by MULTIPLE INVASION; sympatric speciation, by polyploidy (accidental doubling in number of chromosomes in some offspring, which then interbreed among themselves) or by disruptive selection (new selective force splits a previously freely interbreeding population by removing intermediate individuals). Geographic speciation is most common in animals and plants; polyploidy is insignificant in animals, but responsible for the origin of about half of the extant higher plant species; disruptive selection has not been demonstrated.

VICARIANCE. The initiation of SPECIATION and thus CLADOGENESIS by the origin ("vicariance event") of a barrier dividing the range of the parent species. It can be expected to affect a whole number of not necessarily closely related species in the same way.

WILD TYPE. Used by laboratory geneticists to refer to the "normal" allele at the same locus as a conspicuous mutant, or to the normal organism. In other words, the phenotype of a particular organism when first seen in nature.

ZYGOTE. The fertilized ovum of an animal or plant formed from the fusion of male and female gametes.

References

Bagnara, J.T., J. Matsumoto, W. Ferris, S.K. Frost, W.A. Turner, Jr., and J.D. Taylor. 1979. Common origin of pigment cells. Science 203(4379): 410–415.

Brainerd, E.L., S.S. Slutz, E.K. Hall, and R.W. Phillis. 2001. Patterns of genome size evolution in tetraodontiform fishes. Evolution 55(11): 2363–2368.

Britz, R. 1994. Ontogenetic features of *Luciocephalus* (Perciformes, Anabantoidei) with a revised hypothesis of anabantoid intrarelationships. Zoological Journal of the Linnaean Society 112:491–508.

Britz, R. 2001. The genus *Betta*—monophyly and interrelationships, with remarks on the subfamilies Macropodinae and Luciocephalinae (Teleostei: Osphronemidae). Ichthyol. Explor. Freshwaters 12(4):305–318.

Britz, R., and J.A. Cambray. 2001. Structure of egg surfaces and attachment organs in anabantoids. Ichthyol. Explor. Freshwaters 12(3):267–288.

Britz, R., M. Kokoscha, and R. Riehl. 1995. The anabantoid genera *Ctenops, Luciocephalus, Parasphaerichthys*, and *Sphaerichthys* (Teleostei: Perciformes) as a monophyletic group: evidence from egg surface structure and reproductive behavior. Japanese Journal of Ichthyology 42(1):71–79.

Britz, R., and M. Kottelat. 2002. *Parasphaerichthys lineatus*, a new species of labyrinth fish from southern Myanmar (Teleostei: Osphronemidae). Ichthyol. Explor. Freshwaters 13(3): 243–250.

Brock, B.W., N.S. Sodhi, and P.K.L. Ng. 2003. Catastrophic extinctions follow deforestation in Singapore. Nature 424:420–426.

Clark, M., and J. Cummings. 2000. Lonely Planet Guide to Myanmar (Burma), seventh edition, Lonely Planet publications, Melbourne, 480 p.

Cummings, J. 1998. Lonely Planet Guide to Laos, third edition, Lonely Planet publications, Melbourne, 344 p.

Doncaster, C.P. 1997. Lexicon of Evolutionary Genetics. *http://www.geodata.soton.ac.uk/biology/gene.html*

Doncaster, C.P. 2001. Lexicon of Reproductive Modes. *http://www.soton.ac.uk/~cpd/repmod.html*

Donoso, R. 1989. Fischbestandsliste 1/1989. Der Makropode 11(5):71–73.

Donoso, R. 1989. Further notes on *Betta coccina*. Labyrinth, newsletter no. 42, February, 3–9.

Freyhof, J., and F. Herder. 2002. Review of the paradise fishes of the genus Macropodus in Vietnam, with description of two new species from Vietnam and southern China (Perciformes: Osphronemidae). Ichthyol. Explor. Freshwaters 13(2):147–167.

Fujii, R., and N. Oshima. 1986. Control of chromatophore movements in teleost fishes. Zoological Science 3:13–17.

Goldstein, R.J. 2001. *Bettas, A Complete Owner's Manual.* Barron's Educational Series, Hauppauge, NY, 95 pp.

Goldstein, R.J., C. Hopper and G. Pottern. 2000. Report of a chloramine fish kill. Southeastern Society of Parasitologists annual meeting, Chattanooga, TN, abstract.

Hanebuth, T., K. Stategger, and P.M. Grootes. 2000. Rapid flooding of the Sunda Shelf: a late-glacial sea-level record. Science 288:1033–1035.

Hsu, H-M, G.A. Wooster, and P.R. Bowser. 1994. Efficacy of enrofloxacin for the treatment of salmonids with bacterial kidney disease, caused by *Renibacterium salmoninarum.* Journal of Aquatic Animal Health 6:220–223.

Jones, S. 1940. Notes on the breeding habits and early development of *Macropodus cupanus*, with special reference to the cement glands of the early larvae. Records of the Indian Museum 42:269–276.

Kasukawa, H., et al. 1986. Mechanism of light reflection in blue damselfish motile iridophore. Zoological Science 4:243–257.

King, A. A., J. D. Wirtschafter, D. P. Olds, and J. Brumbaugh. 1986. Minimal pigment: a new type of oculocutaneous albinism. Clinical Genetics 29:42–50.

Kottelat, M. 1991. Notes on the taxonomy and distribution of some western Indonesian freshwater fishes, with diagnoses of a new genus and six new species (Pisces: Cyprinidae, Belontiidae, and Chaudhuriidae). Ichthyol. Explor. Freshwaters 2(3):273–287.

Kottelat, M. 1994. Diagnoses of two new species of fighting fishes from Thailand and Cambodia (Teleostei: Belontiidae). Ichthyol. Explor. Freshwaters 5(4):297–304.

Kottelat, M. 2001. *Fishes of Laos.* WHT Publications Ltd., Colombo 5, Sri Lanka. 198 p.

Kottelat, M. 2001. *Freshwater Fishes of Northern Vietnam.* EASES, The World Bank, Washington, D.C., 123 p.

Kottelat, M., and P.K.L. Ng, 1994. Diagnoses of five new species of fighting fishes from Banka and Borneo (Teleostei: Belontiidae). Ichthyol. Explor. Freshwaters 5(1):65–78.

Kottelat, M., and A.J. Whitten, 1996. Freshwater fishes of Western Indonesia and Sulawesi: additions and corrections. Periplus Editions, Hong Kong. 8 p.

Kottelat, M., A.J. Whitten, S.N. Kartikasari, and S. Wirjoatmodjo, 1993. Freshwater fishes of Western Indonesia and Sulawesi. Periplus Editions, Hong Kong. 221 p.

Ladich, F., and H.Y. Yan. 1998. Correlation between auditory sensitivity and vocalization in anabantoid fishes. Journal of Comparative Physiology A. 182:737–746.

Lim, K.K.P., and P.K.L. Ng. 1990. A guide to the freshwater fishes of Singapore. Singapore Science Centre, Science Centre Boulevard, Singapore 22060, 160 pp.

Linke, H. 1989. *Betta foerschi* — Schaumnesterbauer oder Maulbruter? Der Makropode 10(3):34–36.

Linke, H. 1991. *Labyrinth Fish, The Bubble-Nest-Builders*, Tetra (Division of Warner-Lambert), Morris Plains, NJ, 174 pp.

Lom, J., I. Dykova, K. Tonguthai, and S. Chinabut. 1993. Muscle Infection due to *Heterosporis* sp. in the Siamese fighting fish, *Betta splendens* Regan. Journal of Fish Diseases 16(5): 513–516.

Lucas, G. 1980. On the history of bettas. Freshwater and Marine Aquarium 3(9):50 ff.

Lucas, G. 1983. On sex reversal in *Betta splendens*: Is sex ever a sure thing? Freshwater and Marine Aquarium 6(1):26–28, 70–75.

Lucas, G. 1990. Comments on genetic symbolism and symbols used in *Betta* genetics. Freshwater and Marine Aquarium 13(7):66–84.

Mabee, P.M., D.S. Cua, S.B. Barlow, and J.V. Helvik. 1998. Morphology of the hatching glands in *Betta splendens*. Copeia 1998(4):1021–1026.

Martin-Smith, K.M., and H.H. Tan, 1998. Diversity of freshwater fishes from eastern Sabah: annotated checklist for Danum valley and a consideration of inter- and intra-catchment variability. Raffles Bull. Zool. 46(2):573–604.

Matsumoto, J. 1965. Studies on fine structure and cytochemical properties of erythrophores in swordtail, *Xiphophorus helleri*, with special reference to their pigment granules (pterinosomes). Journal of Cell Biology 27(3):493–504.

Ng, P.K.L., and M. Kottelat, 1992. *Betta livida*, a new fighting fish (Teleostei: Belontiidae) from blackwater swamps in peninsular Malaysia. Ichthyol. Explor. Freshwaters 3(2):177–182.

Ng, P.K.L. 1993. On a new species of *Betta* (Teleostei: Belontiidae) from peat swamps in Sabah, East Malaysia, Borneo. Ichthyol. Explor. Freshwaters 4(4):289–294.

Ng, P.K.L., and M. Kottelat, 1994. Revision of the *Betta waseri* species group (Teleostei: Belontiidae). Raffles Bull. Zool. 42(3):593–611.

Norris, S. M. 1995. *Microctenopoma uelense* and *M. nigricans*, a new genus and two new species of anabantid fishes from Africa. Ichthyol. Explor. Freshwaters 6(4): 357–376.

Oshima, N., M. Sato, T. Kumazawa, N. Okeda, H. Kasukawa, and R. Fujii. 1985. Motile iridophores play the leading role in damselfish coloration, pp. 241–246, in, Bagnara, J., S. N. Klaus, E. Paul, and M. Scharti, editors. *Biological, Molecular and Clinical Aspects of Pigmentation*. Pigment Cell 1985, University of Tokyo Press, Tokyo.

Padmanabhan, K. G. 1955. Breeding habits and early embryology of *Macropodus cupanus*. Bulletin of the Central Research Institute, University of Travancore, Trivandrum, series C, 4(1):1–46.

Pinter, H. 1984. *Labyrinth Fish*. Barron's Educational Series, Woodbury, NY, 144 pp.

Pinto, T. 1999. *Betta dimidiata* — luck the second time around. Belontid 1(1):3–5.

Pinto, T. 2000. *Betta persephone*. Osphronemid 2(1):3–5.

Rainboth, W.J. 1996. Fishes of the Cambodian Mekong. FAO Species Identification Field Guide for Fishery Purposes. FAO, Rome, 265 p.

Redweik, C. undated. Kampffische—Nomen ist nicht immer Omen Erfahrungen mit Betta picta und Betta balunga. *http://www.scalare-fulda.de/redweik1.html.*

Rehwinkel, J. Undated. Care and breeding of Betta balunga Herre, 1940. *http://iglnl.netfirms.com/Artikelen/Betta_balunga_artikel/betta_balunga_artikel.htm.*

Richter, H-J. 1981. Ein notwendiger Schritt-Einfuhrung eines neuen Gattungssnamens for die Maulbrutenden Kampffische unter besonderer Betrachtung von *Pseudobetta pugnax* (Cantor, 1849). Aquarien Terrarien (August): 272–325.

Richter, H-J. 1983. *Das Buch der Labyrinth-fische.* Verlag J. Neumann-Neudamm, Berlin, 167 pp.

Roberts, T.R. 1989. The freshwater fishes of western Borneo (Kalimantan Barat, Indonesia). Memoir 14, California Academy of Sciences, San Francisco, CA, 210 pp.

Roberts, T.R. 1992. Systematic revision of the Southeast Asian anabantoid fish genus *Osphronemus*, with descriptions of two new species. Ichthyol. Explor. Freshwaters 2(4): 351–360.

Roloff, E. 1957. *Betta taeniata* Regan. Aquarium Journal 28(12):430–434.

Royal, B. K. 1970. Analysis of red and yellow pigments in two mutants of the Siamese fighting fish, *Betta splendens*. Master's thesis, Biology Department, Drake University, 91 pp.

Royal, B. K. 1976. Isolation and identification of the abnormal opaque material in the white mutant of Siamese fighting fish, *Betta splendens*. Master's thesis, Chemistry Department, Drake University, 73 pp.

Royal, B. K., and G. A. Lucas. 1972–1973. Analysis of red and yellow pigments in two mutants of the Siamese fighting fish, *Betta splendens*. Proceedings of the Iowa Academy of Sciences 79(1972–1973):34–37.

Schäfer, F. 1997. All Labyrinths: bettas, gourami, snakeheads, nandids. Aqualog. A.C.S. Glaser Verlag, Germany, 142 pp.

Schmidt, J. 1992. Brown's fighting fish, another jewel in red and blue. Labyrinth no. 66, pp. 1–6.

Song, J.K., H.Y. Yan, and A. N. Popper. 1995. Damage and recovery of hair cells in fish canal (but not superficial) neuromasts after gentamicin exposure. Hearing Research 91:63–71.

Tan, H.H., 1998. Description of two new species of the *Betta waseri* group (Teleostei: Osphronemidae). Ichthyol. Explor. Freshwaters 8(3):281–287.

Tan, H.H., and M. Kottelat. 1998a. Two new species of *Betta* (Teleostei: Osphronemidae) from the Kapuas Basin, Kalimantan Barat, Borneo. Raffles Bulletin of Zoology 46(1):41–51.

Tan, H.H., and M. Kottelat. 1998b. Redescription of *Betta picta* (Teleostei: Osphronemidae) and description of *B. falx* sp.n. from central Sumatra. Revue Suisse de Zoologie 105(3): 557–568.

Tan, H.H., and P.K.L. Ng. 1996. Redescription of *Betta bellica* Sauvage, 1884, with description of a new allied species from Sumatra. Raffles Bulletin of Zoology 44(1):143–155.

Tan, H.H. and S.H. Tan, 1994. *Betta miniopinna*, a new species of fighting fish from Pulau Bintan, Riau Archipelago,

Indonesia (Teleostei: Belontiidae). Ichthyol. Explor. Freshwaters 5(1):41–44.

Tan, S.H. and H.H. Tan, 1994. The freshwater fishes of Palau Bintan, Riau Archipelago, Sumatra, Indonesia. Tropical Biodiversity 2(3):351.

Tan, H.H., and S.H. Tan. 1996. Redescription of the Malaysian fighting fish *Betta pugnax* (Teleostei: Belontiidae), and description of *Betta pulchra*, new species from peninsular Malaysia. Raffles Bulletin of Zoology 44(2): 419–434.

Turner, P., M. Cambon, B. Delahunty, P. Greenway, and E. Miller. Indonesia, sixth edition. 2000. Lonely Planet Publications, Melbourne, Oakland, London, Paris, 1104 p.

Van Der Voort, S. 2003. *Betta* cf. *burdigala* "Kubu." Osphronemid 5(2):15–18.

Voris, H.K. 2000. Maps of Pleistocene sea levels in southeast Asia: shorelines, river systems, and time durations. Biogeography 27:1153–1167.

Wang, J. 2002. An estimator for pairwise relatedness using molecular markers. J. Genetics 160:1203–1215.

Wede, I., A.A. Altindag, B. Widner, H. Wachter, and D. Fuchs. 1998. Inhibition of xanthine oxidase by pterins. Free Radical Research 29(4):331–338.

Witte, K-E., and J. Schmidt. 1992. *Betta brownorum*, a new species of anabantoids (Teleostei: Belontiidae) from northwestern Borneo, with a key to the genus. Ichthyol. Explor. Freshwaters, 2(4):305–330.

Yan, H.Y. Auditory role of the suprabranchial chamber in gourami fish. Journal of Comparative Physiology A. 183:325–333.

Non-profit Sources of Wild and Fancy Bettas

International Betta Congress (IBC)	*www.ibcbettas.org*
International Anabantoid Association (IAA)	*mjanson@wi.rrl.com*
Anabantoid Association of Great Britain	*cj@labyrinth5.fsnet.co.uk*
French Anabantoid Association	*marcmaurin@free.fr*

Commercial Sources of Fancy Bettas

Betta Labs	*www.bettalabs.com*
Aqua Bid	*www.aquabid.com*
The Betta Cave	*www.bettacave.com*
BC Betta	*www.bcbetta.com*
Sunpetch Panasjaroen	*http://bbests.s5.com/mainpage.htm*
Betta Starz	*www.bettastarz.com*
The Fish Wizards	*www.thefishwizards.com/html/ fish4sale.htm*
EBetta2U	*www.ebetta2u.com*
Atison Phumchoosri Betta Farm	*www.atisonbetta.com*
Fish Link Central	*www.fishlinkcentral.com/links/ commercial/breeders/bettas/*

Index